Hands-On Data Science with the Command Line

Automate everyday data science tasks using command-line tools

Jason Morris
Chris McCubbin
Raymond Page

BIRMINGHAM - MUMBAI

Hands-On Data Science with the Command Line

Copyright © 2019 Packt Publishing

All rights reserved. No part of this book may be reproduced, stored in a retrieval system, or transmitted in any form or by any means, without the prior written permission of the publisher, except in the case of brief quotations embedded in critical articles or reviews.

Every effort has been made in the preparation of this book to ensure the accuracy of the information presented. However, the information contained in this book is sold without warranty, either express or implied. Neither the authors, nor Packt Publishing or its dealers and distributors, will be held liable for any damages caused or alleged to have been caused directly or indirectly by this book.

Packt Publishing has endeavored to provide trademark information about all of the companies and products mentioned in this book by the appropriate use of capitals. However, Packt Publishing cannot guarantee the accuracy of this information.

Acquisition Editor: Divya Poojari
Content Development Editor: Mohammed Yusuf Imaratwale
Technical Editor: Diksha Wakode
Copy Editor: Safis Editing
Project Coordinator: Kinjal Bari
Proofreader: Safis Editing
Indexer: Tejal Daruwale Soni
Graphics: Jason Monteiro
Production Coordinator: Arvindkumar Gupta

First published: January 2019
Production reference: 1310119

Published by Packt Publishing Ltd.
Livery Place
35 Livery Street
Birmingham
B3 2PB, UK.

ISBN 978-1-78913-298-4

www.packtpub.com

mapt.io

Mapt is an online digital library that gives you full access to over 5,000 books and videos, as well as industry leading tools to help you plan your personal development and advance your career. For more information, please visit our website.

Why subscribe?

- Spend less time learning and more time coding with practical eBooks and Videos from over 4,000 industry professionals
- Improve your learning with Skill Plans built especially for you
- Get a free eBook or video every month
- Mapt is fully searchable
- Copy and paste, print, and bookmark content

Packt.com

Did you know that Packt offers eBook versions of every book published, with PDF and ePub files available? You can upgrade to the eBook version at `www.packt.com` and as a print book customer, you are entitled to a discount on the eBook copy. Get in touch with us at `customercare@packtpub.com` for more details.

At `www.packt.com`, you can also read a collection of free technical articles, sign up for a range of free newsletters, and receive exclusive discounts and offers on Packt books and eBooks.

Contributors

About the authors

Jason Morris is a systems and research engineer with over 19 years of experience in system architecture, research engineering, and large data analysis. His primary focus is machine learning with TensorFlow, CUDA, and Apache Spark.

Jason is also a speaker and a consultant on designing large-scale architectures, implementing best security practices on the cloud, creating near real-time image detection analytics with deep learning, and developing serverless architectures to aid in ETL. His most recent roles include solution architect, big data engineer, big data specialist, and instructor at Amazon Web Services. He is currently the Chief Technology Officer of Next Rev Technologies, and his favorite command-line program is `netcat`.

> *I want to thank the team at Packt Publishing for helping the authors from beginning to end in the writing of this book. To the number of open source developers that helped make the command line what it is today, thank you for all you do. This book wouldn't be possible without you. And to the readers of this publication, may this book aid you in your quest of doing great things.*

Chris McCubbin is a data scientist and software developer with 20 years' experience in developing complex systems and analytics. He co-founded the successful big data security start-up Sqrrl, since acquired by Amazon. He has also developed smart swarming systems for drones, social network analysis systems in MapReduce, and big data security analytic platforms using the Accumulo and Spark Apache projects. He has been using the Unix command line, starting on IRIX platforms in college, and his favorite command-line program is `find`.

> *Thanks to my wife, Angel, for giving me the time to finish this book. Also thanks to Tom Swindell for his help with proofreading and editing.*

Raymond Page is a computer engineer specializing in site reliability. His experience with embedded development engendered a passion for removing the pervasive bloat from web technologies and cloud computing. His favorite command is `cat`.

> *I want to thank Jason and Chris for adding my esoteric shell knowledge to this book, I've had a blast working with them. I also want to thank the entire Packt team for being so helpful throughout the editorial process. To my family, all my love for enduring my absences from game nights and story time to complete this book.*

About the reviewers

Chankey Pathak is a data scientist from India. He's the author of the Python API for high frequency trading of Morgan Stanley. He has worked with Citadel, Sophos, and Proofpoint in the past. He's also well known in the Perl community for his contributions. He is an open source contributor and loves Linux.

Tom Swindell is a systems engineer with 15 years of experience in software architecture, data analysis, and algorithms. He works for Net Vision Consultants, performing a mix of systems engineering, Python development, and system administration.

Packt is searching for authors like you

If you're interested in becoming an author for Packt, please visit `authors.packtpub.com` and apply today. We have worked with thousands of developers and tech professionals, just like you, to help them share their insight with the global tech community. You can make a general application, apply for a specific hot topic that we are recruiting an author for, or submit your own idea.

Table of Contents

Preface — 1

Chapter 1: Data Science at the Command Line and Setting It Up — 5
   History of the command line — 6
   We don't want to BaSH other shells, but... — 8
   Language-focused shells — 8
   So, why the command line? — 9
   Getting set up with Windows 10 — 11
   Getting set up on OS X — 16
   Getting set up on Ubuntu Linux — 18
      Getting set up with Docker — 19
   Summary — 20

Chapter 2: Essential Commands — 21
   Essential commands — 21
   Navigating the command line — 26
      Getting help — 28
      Customizing the shell — 30
   Summary — 30

Chapter 3: Shell Workflows, and Data Acquisition and Massaging — 31
   Download the data — 32
   Using the file command — 33
   Performing a word count — 35
   Introduction to cut — 37
   Detached processing — 39
      How to background a process — 40
      Disregarding SIGHUP — 41
      Terminal multiplexers — 41
         Introduction to screen — 41
      Sharing a screen session between multiple users — 44
      Introduction to tmux — 44
   Summary — 46

Chapter 4: Bash Functions and Data Visualization — 47
   My first shell script — 48
      She bangs, she bangs! — 48
      Function arguments, positional parameters, and IFS — 49
         Prompt me baby one more time — 49
      Feed the function input! — 51

Table of Contents

Down the rabbit hole of IFS and bash arrays	52
Advanced shell scripting magic	**53**
Here be dragons, ye be warned	53
Text injection of text files	53
Bash networks for fun and profit!	54
From dumb Terminal to glam Terminal	**56**
Who, what, where, why, how?	59
Enter the mind's eye	63
Summary	**66**
Chapter 5: Loops, Functions, and String Processing	**67**
Once, twice, three times a lady loops	**68**
It's the end of the world as we know it while and until	**70**
The simple case	**72**
Pay no heed to the magician redirecting your attention	**73**
Regular expressions and grep	**75**
Exact matches	76
Character sets	76
Dot the i (or anything else)	77
Capture groups	78
Either or, neither nor	78
Repetition	79
Other operators	79
Putting it all together	80
awk, sed, and tr	**80**
awk	80
sed	82
tr	83
sort and uniq	83
sort	83
uniq	85
Summary	**86**
Chapter 6: SQL, Math, and Wrapping it up	**87**
cut and viewing data as columnar	**88**
WHERE clauses	90
Join, for joining data	91
Group by and ordering	92
Simulating selects	**93**
Keys to the kingdom	**94**
Using SQLite	94
Math in bash itself	**96**
Using let	96
Basic arithmetic	96
Double-parentheses	96
bc, the unix basic calculator	97

Math in (g)awk	98
Python (pandas, numpy, scikit-learn)	99
Analyzing weather data in bash	100
Summary	105
Other Books You May Enjoy	107
Index	111

Preface

In this book, we introduce the power of the command line using the bash shell. Bash is the most widely accepted shell, and is found on everything from toasters to high-performance computers. We start with the basics and quickly move to some more advanced skills throughout the book.

Who this book is for

Hands-On Data Science with the Command Line provides useful tips and tricks on how to use the command line for everyday data problems. This book is aimed for the reader that has little to no command-line experience but has worked in the field of computer science and/or has experience with modern data science problems.

You'll learn how to set up the command line on multiple platforms and configure it to your liking, learn how to find help with commands, and learn how to create reusable scripts. You will also learn how to obtain an actual dataset, perform some analytics, and learn how to visualize the data. Towards the end of the book, we touch on some of the advanced features of the command line and where to go from there.

In addition, all of the code examples are available to download in Packt's GitHub account. Any updates to this book will be made available to you by the Packt platform.

What this book covers

Chapter 1, *Data Science at the Command line and Setting It up*, covers how to install and configure the command line on multiple platforms of your choosing.

Chapter 2, *Essential Commands*, is a hands-on demo on using the basics of the command line and where to find help if needed.

Chapter 3, *Shell Workflows, and Data Acquisition and Massaging*, really gets into performing some basic data science exercises with a live dataset and customizing your command-line environment as you see fit.

Chapter 4, *Reusable Bash and Developing Reusable Code in Bash*, builds on the previous chapters and gets more advanced with creating reusable scripts and visualizations.

Preface

Chapter 5, *Loops, Functions, and String Processing*, is an advanced hands-on exercise on iterating over data using loops and exploring with regular expressions.

Chapter 6, *SQL, Math, and Wrapping it up*, is an advanced hands-on exercise to use what you've learned over the last chapters, and we introduce databases, streaming, and working with APIs.

To get the most out of this book

For this book, all you require is the Bash shell and a operating system that can run the command line or the latest version of Docker. You will also need an Internet connection (preferably cable or higher) and strong typing skills.

Download the example code files

You can download the example code files for this book from your account at www.packt.com. If you purchased this book elsewhere, you can visit www.packt.com/support and register to have the files emailed directly to you.

You can download the code files by following these steps:

1. Log in or register at www.packt.com.
2. Select the **SUPPORT** tab.
3. Click on **Code Downloads & Errata**.
4. Enter the name of the book in the **Search** box and follow the onscreen instructions.

Once the file is downloaded, please make sure that you unzip or extract the folder using the latest version of:

- WinRAR/7-Zip for Windows
- Zipeg/iZip/UnRarX for Mac
- 7-Zip/PeaZip for Linux

The code bundle for the book is also hosted on GitHub at https://github.com/PacktPublishing/Hands-On-Data-Science-with-Command-Line. In case there's an update to the code, it will be updated on the existing GitHub repository.

We also have other code bundles from our rich catalog of books and videos available at https://github.com/PacktPublishing/. Check them out!

Conventions used

There are a number of text conventions used throughout this book.

`CodeInText`: Indicates code words in text, database table names, folder names, filenames, file extensions, pathnames, dummy URLs, user input, and Twitter handles. Here is an example: "Mount the downloaded `WebStorm-10*.dmg` disk image file as another disk in your system."

A block of code is set as follows:

```
<<EOF cat >greetlib.sh
greet_yourself () {
    echo Hello, \${1:-\$USER}!
}
EOF
```

When we wish to draw your attention to a particular part of a code block, the relevant lines or items are set in bold:

```
<key>Ctrl+b</key> "
<key>Ctrl+b</key> <key></key>
<key>Ctrl+b</key> "
```

Any command-line input or output is written as follows:

```
sudo apt install -y screen tmux
```

Bold: Indicates a new term, an important word, or words that you see onscreen. For example, words in menus or dialog boxes appear in the text like this. Here is an example: "Select **System info** from the **Administration** panel."

Warnings or important notes appear like this.

Tips and tricks appear like this.

Get in touch

Feedback from our readers is always welcome.

General feedback: If you have questions about any aspect of this book, mention the book title in the subject of your message and email us at customercare@packtpub.com.

Errata: Although we have taken every care to ensure the accuracy of our content, mistakes do happen. If you have found a mistake in this book, we would be grateful if you would report this to us. Please visit www.packt.com/submit-errata, selecting your book, clicking on the Errata Submission Form link, and entering the details.

Piracy: If you come across any illegal copies of our works in any form on the Internet, we would be grateful if you would provide us with the location address or website name. Please contact us at copyright@packt.com with a link to the material.

If you are interested in becoming an author: If there is a topic that you have expertise in and you are interested in either writing or contributing to a book, please visit authors.packtpub.com.

Reviews

Please leave a review. Once you have read and used this book, why not leave a review on the site that you purchased it from? Potential readers can then see and use your unbiased opinion to make purchase decisions, we at Packt can understand what you think about our products, and our authors can see your feedback on their book. Thank you!

For more information about Packt, please visit packt.com.

Data Science at the Command Line and Setting It Up

"In the beginning... was the command line" Years ago, we didn't have fancy frameworks that handled our distributed computing for us, or applications that could read files intelligently and give us accurate results. If we did, it was very expensive or only worked for a small problem set, very few people had access to this technology, and it was mostly proprietary.

For newcomers to the world of data science, you might have used the command line for a small number of things. Maybe you moved a file from one place to another using mv, or read a file using cat. Or you might have never used the command line at all, or at least not for data science. In this book, we hope to show you a number of tools and ways you can perform some everyday tasks that you can do locally, without using today's buzzword framework.

We created this book for the folks who have little to no experience with the command line, and perform a lot of data extraction, modelling, parsing, and analyzing. This doesn't mean that if you do have a lot of command-line experience (a lot of DevOps and systems folks do), you shouldn't read this book. In fact, you might pick up a couple commands and techniques that you haven't used before.

In this chapter, we will cover the following topics:

- The history of the command line
- Language-focused shells
- Why use the command line?

We will also walk through the setup and configuration of the command line with the following operating systems:

- Windows 10
- Mac OS X
- Ubuntu Linux

If you are running a different operating system, we suggest obtaining an instance from a cloud provider or using the Docker container that's provided in this book.

History of the command line

Since the very first electronic machines, people have strived to communicate with them the same way that we humans talk to each other. But since natural-language processing was beyond the technological grasp of early computer systems, engineers relatively quickly replaced the punch cards, dials, and knobs of early computing machines with teletypes: typewriter-like machines that enabled keyed input and textual output to a display. Teletypes were replaced fairly quickly with video monitors, enabling a world of graphical displays. A novelty of the time, teletypes served a function that was missing in graphical environments, and thus terminal emulators were born for serving as the modern interface to the command line. The programs behind the terminals started out as an ingrained part of the computer itself: resident monitor programs that were able to start a job, detect when it was done, and clean up.

As computers grew in complexity, so did the programs controlling them. Resident monitors gave way to operating systems that were able to share time between multiple jobs. In the early 1960s, Louis Pouzin had the brilliant idea to use the commands being fed to the computer as a kind of program, a *shell* around the operating system.

"After having written dozens of commands for CTSS, I reached the stage where I felt that commands should be usable as building blocks for writing more commands, just like subroutine libraries. Hence, I wrote RUNCOM, a sort of shell that drives the execution of command scripts, with argument substitution. The tool became instantly popular, as it became possible to go home in the evening and leaving long runcoms to execute overnight."

Scripting in this way, and the reuse of tooling, would become an ingrained trope in the exciting new world of programmable computing. Pouzin's concepts for a programmable shell made their way into the design and philosophy of Multics in the 1960s and its Bell Labs successor, Unix.

In the Bell System Technical Journal from 1978, Doug McIlroy wrote the following regarding the Unix system:

> "A number of maxims have gained currency among the builders and users of the UNIX system to explain and promote its characteristic style: Make each program do one thing well. To do a new job, build afresh rather than complicate old programs by adding new features."

- Expect the output of every program to become the input to another, as yet unknown, program. Don't clutter output with extraneous information. Avoid stringently columnar or binary input formats. Don't insist on interactive input.
- Design and build software, even operating systems, to be tried early, ideally within weeks. Don't hesitate to throw away the clumsy parts and rebuild them.
- Use tools in preference to unskilled help to lighten a programming task, even if you have to detour to build the tools and expect to throw some of them out after you've finished using them.

This is the core of the Unix philosophy and the key tenets that make the command line not just a way to launch programs or list files, but a powerful group of community-built tools that can work together to process data in a clean, simple manner. In fact, McIlroy follows up with this great example of how this had led to success with data processing, even back in 1978:

> "Unexpected uses of files abound: programs may be compiled to be run and also typeset to be published in a book from the same text without human intervention; text intended for publication serves as grist for statistical studies of English to help in data compression or cryptography; mailing lists turn into maps. The prevalence of free-format text, even in "data" files, makes the text-processing utilities useful for many strictly data processing functions such as shuffling fields, counting, or collating."

Having access to simple yet powerful components, programmers needed an easy way to construct, reuse, and execute more complicated commands and scripts to do the processing specific to their needs. Enter the early fully-featured command line shell: the Bourne shell. Developed by Stephen Bourne (also at Bell Labs) in the late 1970s for Unix's System 7, the Bourne shell was designed from the start with programmers like us in mind: it had all the scripting tools needed to put the community-developed single-purpose tools to good use. It was the right tool, in the right place, at the right time; almost all Unix systems today are based upon System 7 and nearly all still include the original Bourne shell as an option. In this book, we will use a descendant of the venerable Bourne shell, known as Bash, which is a rewrite of the Bourne shell released in 1989 for the GNU project that incorporated the best features of the Bourne shell itself along with several of its earlier spinoffs.

We don't want to BaSH other shells, but...

In this book, we decided to focus on using the **Bourne-again shell** (**bash**) for multiple reasons. First, it's the most popular shell and you can find it everywhere. In fact, for the majority of Linux distributions, bash is the default shell. It's a great first shell to learn and very easy to work with. There's a number of examples and resources available to help you with bash if you ever get stuck. It's also safe to say that since it's so popular, you can find it on almost any system available today. From a bare-metal installation in a data center to an instance running in the cloud, bash is there, installed, and waiting for input.

There are a number of other shells you can choose from, such as the Z shell (zsh). The Z shell is fairly new (and by new I mean released in 1990, which is new in shell land) and provides a number of powerful features. Other notable shells are tcsh, ksh, and fish. The C Shell (tcsh), the Korn Shell (ksh), and the **Friendly Interactive Shell** (**fish**) are still widely used today. FreeBSD has made tcsh its default shell for the root user and ksh is still used for a lot of Solaris operating systems. Fish is also a great starter shell with a lot of features to help the user navigate the shell without feeling lost.

While these shells are still very powerful and stable, we will be focusing on using bash, as we want to focus on consistency across multiple platforms and help you learn a very active and popular shell that's been around for 30 years.

Language-focused shells

As a data scientist, I'm sure you do a lot of work with Python and Scala or have at least heard of those two languages. Two of our favorite shell replacements are Xonsh and Ammonite. Xonsh (https://xon.sh/) is a Python-powered shell that uses Python 3.4, and Ammonite (http://ammonite.io/) is a Scala-powered shell that uses Scala 2.11.7 (both versions are at time of writing). If you find yourself using a lot of Python or Scala in your day-to-day work, we recommend checking those shell replacements out as well after you've mastered the command line using bash.

So, why the command line?

As the field of data science is still fairly new (it used to be called **operations research**), the tools and frameworks are also fairly new. With that being said, the command line is almost 50 years old and still one of the most powerful tools used today. If you're familiar with interpreters, the command line will come easy to you. Think of it as a place to experiment and see your results in real time. Every command you enter is executed interactively, and when you call a bash script to run, it executes sequentially (unless you decide not to, more in later chapters). As we know, experimenting and exploring is most of what data science tries to accomplish (and it's the most fun!).

I was having a conversation with a newly-graduated data science student about parsing text and asked, "How would you take a small file and provide a word count on how many time the words appear?" By now everyone is familiar with the infamous Hadoop word-count example. It's considered the "Hello, World" of data science.

The answer I received was a little shocking but expected. The student instantly replied that they'd use Hadoop to read the file, tokenize the words to form a key/value pair, reduce all the keys and values that are grouped together, and add up the occurrences. The student isn't wrong, in fact, that's a perfectly acceptable answer. Especially if the file is too large for a single system (big data), you already have the code in place to scale.

With that being said, what if I told you there's a quicker way to obtain the results that doesn't require programming in Java and setting up a cluster or having Hadoop run locally? In fact, it would only take one line to complete the task? Check out the following code:

```
cat file.txt | tr '[:space:]' '[\n*]' | grep -v "^$" | sort | uniq -c | sort -bnr
(tr '[:space:]' '[\n*]' | grep -v "^$" | sort | uniq -c | sort -bnr
)<file.txt
```

This may seem like a lot, especially if you've never used the command line before, so let's break it down. The `cat` command reads files sequentially and writes them to standard output. `|`, also known as pipe or the pipe operator, combines a sequence of commands chained together by their standard streams so that the output of each process (`stdout`) feeds directly as input (`stdin`) to the next one. `tr` (translate) reads the input from `cat` (via `|`) and writes the result to standard output that replaces spaces with new lines. The `grep` command is very powerful and the most used for a lot of data parsing. `grep` is used to search plain-text data for lines that match a regular expression. In this example, `grep` trims out the empty lines. `sort` is used for, well, sorting! You'll notice a lot of the commands are named for what they actually do. The `sort` command prints the lines of its input or concatenation of files listed in its argument list in sorted order. `uniq` is a command that, when fed a text file, outputs the file with adjacent identical lines collapsed to one. It usually works well with the `sort` command. In this example, `uniq -c` is called to count occurrences. And finally, `sort -bnr` sorts in numeric reverse order and ignores whitespace.

Don't worry if the example looks foreign to you. The command line also comes with manual pages for each command. All you have to do is `man` the command to view the page. You can even `man man` to get an idea of what the `man` command does! Give it a whirl and `man tr` or `man sort`. Oh, you don't have the command line set up? It's easier than you think, and we can get you up in running in minutes, so let's get started.

Chapter 1

Getting set up with Windows 10

We want the readers to keep in mind that PowerShell will not work with the examples listed in this book. However, Microsoft has seen fit to release their Windows Subsystem for Linux as of Windows 10 version 1607 and later. It's also easy to install: open the Microsoft Store, search for Ubuntu (a Linux distribution), and install it:

[11]

Data Science at the Command Line and Setting It Up

In Windows 10 version 1607 and later, you have the ability to run Linux natively with your choice of distribution. In this example, we will use Ubuntu on top of Windows 10 to get our workspace set up. Make sure you have the latest version of Windows installed in order to take advantage of WSL (Windows Subsystem for Linux); at a minimum, you need the Windows 10 Fall Creator update to proceed. Also keep in mind that WSL is in beta at the time of writing. If you don't feel comfortable installing beta software, I recommend finding an alternative, such as an EC2 instance on AWS, or skipping ahead to the *Docker* section of this book:

1. Go to the Start menu and search for PowerShell:

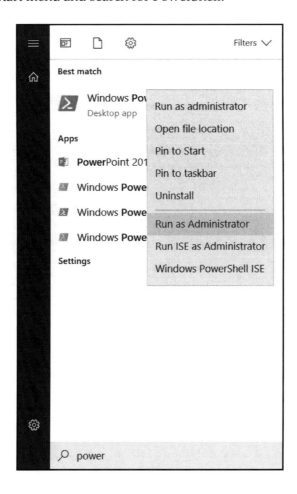

2. Double-click **Windows PowerShell** and click **Run as Administrator**.
3. Type the following command to enable WSL:

   ```
   Enable-WindowsOptionalFeature -Online -FeatureName Microsoft-Windows-Subsystem-Linux
   ```

   The following should be displayed:

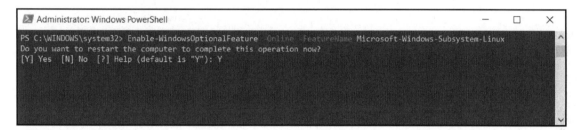

4. You will be asked to confirm your choice. Use *Y* or press *Enter*:

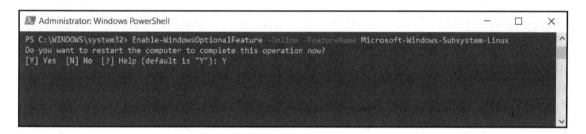

5. Press *Y* to reboot.

Once your system has rebooted, do the following:

1. Go to the Start menu and search for Store.
2. Search for Ubuntu:

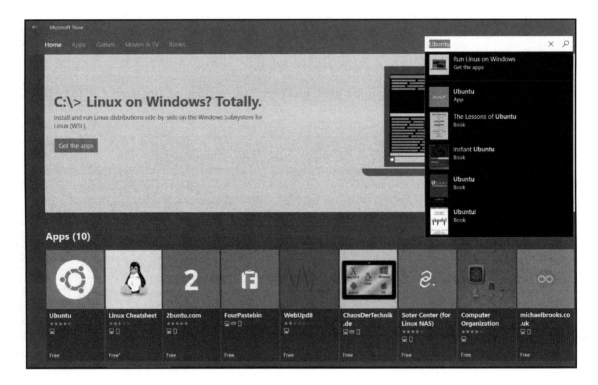

3. Click **Install**:

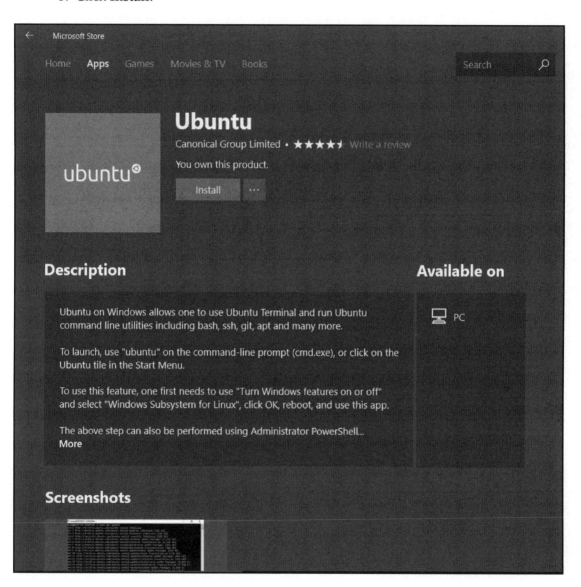

Data Science at the Command Line and Setting It Up

4. Click **Launch**.
5. When asked to create a username and password, go ahead and create one. Make sure you remember this information as you'll need it throughout this book:

```
Installing, this may take a few minutes...
Installation successful!
Please create a default UNIX user account. The username does not need to match your Windows username.
For more information visit: https://aka.ms/wslusers
Enter new UNIX username: jason
Enter new UNIX password:
Retype new UNIX password:
passwd: password updated successfully
Default UNIX user set to: jason
To run a command as administrator (user "root"), use "sudo <command>".
See "man sudo_root" for details.
```

6. Success! You now have completed the setup and installation of Linux on Windows 10.

Install the following tools as we will be using them throughout this book:

```
sudo apt update
sudo apt install jq python-pip gnuplot sqlite3 libsqlite3-dev curl netcat bc
pip install pandas
```

Getting set up on OS X

OS X already has a full command-line system installed using bash as the default shell. To access this shell, click the magnifying glass in the upper-right corner and type `terminal` in the dialog box:

This will open a bash Terminal:

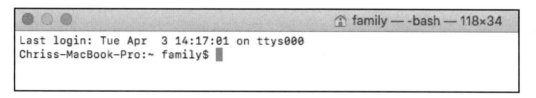

As in other bash shells, this Terminal doesn't have everything installed, so type the following commands to install the requisite installers and command-line tools that we'll be using in this book:

```
/usr/bin/ruby -e "$(curl -fsSL
https://raw.githubusercontent.com/Homebrew/install/master/install)"
brew install jq sqlite gnuplot python netcat bc
pip3 install pandas
```

On OS X, this script installs a few installation tools, including `pip` and `homebrew`. It then uses these tools to install the commands that we use in this book that aren't natively installed, namely `jq`, `gnuplot`, `sqlite`, and `pandas`.

One thing to look out for in OS X is that certain standard tools are built a little differently than the ones that come with Debian-based systems like the rest of the systems we talk about in this chapter. In some circumstances, OS X tools work slightly differently or have different options. Where this is the case we have noted it in the text.

Getting set up on Ubuntu Linux

Ubuntu has a full built-in command-line shell and typically uses bash as the default shell. Different window managers have slightly different ways of opening a Terminal window. For example, in the image of Ubuntu 17.10 Artful (located at https://www.osboxes.org/ubuntu/), open the Terminal by clicking on **Activities** in the upper-left corner and typing `terminal` in the dialog:

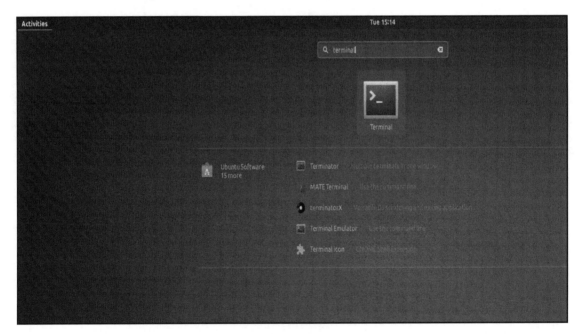

This will bring up a command-line prompt:

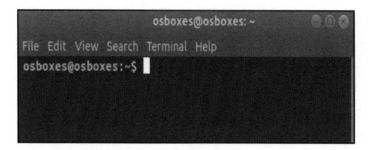

As in other bash shells, this shell doesn't have everything installed, so type the following command to install the installers and command-line tools that we will use in this book:

```
sudo apt update
sudo apt install jq python-pip gnuplot sqlite3 libsqlite3-dev curl netcat bc
pip install pandas
```

On Ubuntu, this script installs a few installation tools, including pip. It then uses these tools to install the commands that we use in this book that aren't natively installed, namely `jq`, `gnuplot`, `sqlite`, `curl`, and `pandas`.

Getting set up with Docker

What if there were a way to obtain an image with all the commands preinstalled and you were able to run it on most major operating systems without any issues? That's exactly what Docker provides, and you can quickly get up and running in a matter of minutes:

1. Visit `https://www.docker.com/community-edition` and install the version of Docker for your operating system
2. Run the following command to obtain the Docker image:

   ```
   docker run -ivt nextrevtech/commandline-book /bin/bash
   ```

Summary

The command line has a long history, and it can be quite foreign to newcomers. In this chapter, we covered the environment setup steps so that you can follow along with the examples in this book. Essential commands will introduce what you need to succeed, followed by acquiring datasets that we can play with. We will cover all the shell magic, such as background processes, writing shell functions, basic shell control-flow constructs, visualizing results, processing strings, simulating database functionality, simple math constructs, and finally a synthesis of all of these in a penultimate chapter of magical fascination.

Everything you need to explore the rest of the book is now installed and configured. As you saw, the command line can run on pretty much anything, which makes it an invaluable tool to have in your toolkit.

In the next chapter, we will use our newly-installed command-line environment to run some essential commands, learn how to customize the shell, and look at how to use the built-in help when we get stuck.

2
Essential Commands

Now that we have the command line set up and installed, we will go over a list of everyday commands that are considered the basics. Having a fundamental understanding of the basic commands will be the building block on which we'll learn the advanced commands found later in this book.

In this chapter, we will cover the following topics:

- Basic command-line navigation
- Redirecting input and output
- Where to get help if you're stuck
- How to customize the shell to your liking

Essential commands

Woah... hold your horses, we need to cover some basics about commands. A command is a process run by a **POSIX** (**Portable Operating System Interface**) compliant **OS** (**Operating System**). OpenGroup maintains the standard in addition to it being ratified as an IEEE standard (http://pubs.opengroup.org/onlinepubs/9699919799/). In a POSIX environment, the process being run will have an environment, a current working directory, the command line (the path name that invoked the command and any arguments), and a series of file descriptors with `stdin`, `stdout`, and `stderr` (referred to by integer numbers 0, 1, and 2, respectively) being connected prior to handoff to your command.

Now with a little background and an installed command line, you are ready to go and we can actually start running commands. We will be going over some basic everyday commands. For those that are ready to delve in, let's discuss how we locate the commands we can run.

Essential Commands

Locating commands is akin to searching through a filing cabinet, what we call a filesystem. Commands are just files stored in the filing cabinet, and folders or directories are used to organize the files into a hierarchy. Each directory may contain many files or other directories, and has a single parent directory. To open our filing cabinet, we need to start at the top of the hierarchy, the root directory, /. The first set of commands you need to know involve commands to traverse the filesystem and get your bearings.

When you log into the command line, it's likely that you will be in your home directory. What this directory is varies by system. To see where you are, try the pwd (present working directory) command:

> **pwd**

The following is what you should see on running the preceding command:

Here, ubuntu is your username. This means you are currently in the ubuntu directory, which is in the home directory, /. From here, if you try to open a file with a relative path name, that is, one that doesn't start with a /, the command line will look for that file in your current directory (you can do things with files in other directories without changing your current one, we will talk about that in a bit).

You might want to create your own directories. To do this, we can try the following command:

> **mkdir foo**

The following is what you should see on running the preceding command:

Which makes the directory foo inside your current directory. If this command completes successfully, it won't print anything. To see the directory we just made, we use the list command:

> **ls**

The following is what you should see on running the preceding command:

```
ubuntu@commandlinebook:~$ pwd
/home/ubuntu
ubuntu@commandlinebook:~$
```

It should be on a line by itself. We might want to print a little bit more information about the directory. In this case, we can pass some flags to the `ls` command to alter what it's doing. For example, type the following:

```
ls -l
```

This is what you should see on running the preceding command:

```
ubuntu@commandlinebook:~$ ls -l
total 4
drwxrwxr-x 2 ubuntu ubuntu 4096 Jun 23 23:57 foo
ubuntu@commandlinebook:~$
```

It's not too important right now to understand everything printed here, but we can see that foo is a directory, not a data file (from the d code in the front), and the date and time it was created. This is a common pattern among UNIX commands. The default version of the command does one thing, and passing in flags like -l.

Sometimes, commands have arguments, and sometimes flags of commands will have arguments, too. A general form of a command might appear as follows:

```
<command> -a <argument> -b -c -d <argument> <command arguments>
```

Here, a, b, c, and d are flags of the command. What exactly these commands are, and what they do, are dependent on the command.

Let's go into our newly-created directory and mess around with some data files:

```
cd foo
```

The following is what you should see on running the preceding command:

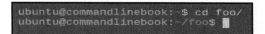

Essential Commands

The `cd` (or change directory) command changes your current working directory. Let's now string together two commands to create a data file. We will talk about this a bit later, but for now we just need a file to mess around with:

```
echo "Hello world..." > hello.txt
```

The following is what you should see on running the preceding command:

```
ubuntu@commandlinebook:~/foo$ echo "Hello world..." > hello.txt
ubuntu@commandlinebook:~/foo$
```

This won't produce any output, but it will create a file called `hello.txt` (as we told the shell to redirect `stdout` with > to a file) that contains the single line of **Hello world...** text. To see this, we can use the concatenate command:

```
cat hello.txt
```

The following is what you should see on running the preceding command:

```
ubuntu@commandlinebook:~/foo$ cat hello.txt
"Hello world..."
ubuntu@commandlinebook:~/foo$
```

This will print the contents of any file. If we only want to see the first, or last, few lines of a file, we could use `head` and `tail` instead of `cat`.

If this all sounds pretty simple, there's a good reason: each command in UNIX is intended to do one thing and do it well. Often options can be used to tailor a command's behavior. The really neat stuff you can do starts to happen when we start tying commands together using pipes and redirection.

You see, almost every command in UNIX has some way to input data into it. The command then takes the input, and, depending on its parameters and flags, transforms that input into something else and outputs it. We can use the pipe, |, to take the output from one command, and feed it into the input of another command. This simple but extremely powerful idea will let us do a lot with a few commands.

Let's try a simple example: let's use `echo`, with the `-e` flag, to tell it to pay attention to control characters, to make a multi-line file (by using the `\n`) with some numbers on each line.

```
echo -e "1\n3\n19\n1\n25\n5" > numbers.txt
cat numbers.txt
```

The following is what you should see on running the preceding command:

```
ubuntu@commandlinebook:~/foo$ echo -e "1\n3\n19\n1\n25\n5" > numbers.txt
ubuntu@commandlinebook:~/foo$ cat numbers.txt
1
3
19
1
25
5
ubuntu@commandlinebook:~/foo$
```

Now, say we wanted to see those numbers sorted. The sort command does just this. Using a flag to sort to consider the lines to be numbers and not strings, we can pipe the output of cat into the sort function:

`cat numbers.txt | sort -n`

The following is what you should see on running the preceding command:

```
ubuntu@commandlinebook:~/foo$ cat numbers.txt | sort -n
1
1
3
5
19
25
ubuntu@commandlinebook:~/foo$
```

If we then want to see just the unique numbers in sorted order, we can re-pipe this output to the uniq command, which returns unique lines from the given input:

`cat numbers.txt | sort -n | uniq`

The following is what you should see on running the preceding command:

```
ubuntu@commandlinebook:~/foo$ cat numbers.txt | sort -n | uniq
1
3
5
19
25
ubuntu@commandlinebook:~/foo$
```

Essential Commands

And so on, and so on. We can build up the pipeline we want a bit at a time, debugging along the way. You will see this technique throughout this book.

One last thing: in some of these commands, we have seen the >, or redirect. Redirection can be used for a number of things, but most of the time it's used to redirect the output of a command to a file:

```
<some pipeline of commands>  > <filename>
```

This will replace the contents of the file named filename with the output of the pipeline.

With these simple tools, you have enough to get started hacking data with bash.

Navigating the command line

There's a couple of useful tricks for navigating the command line that, while optional, will improve your quality of life. This section has a selection of those tricks.

Bash, by default, saves the history of your commands. It will even save the history across sessions. This can be extremely useful because sometimes we make a small mistake and don't want to retype an entire command, or we want to repeat the same commands over and over. To see your history, type this command:

```
history
```

The following is what you should see on running the preceding command:

```
ubuntu@commandlinebook:~/foo$ history
    1  pwd
    2  mkdir foo
    3  ls
    4  ls -l
    5  cd foo/
    6  echo "Hello world..." > hello.txt
    7  cat hello.txt
    8  echo -e "1\n3\n19\n1\n25\n5" > numbers.txt
    9  cat numbers.txt
   10  cat numbers.txt | sort -n
   11  cat numbers.txt | sort -n | uniq
   12  history
ubuntu@commandlinebook:~/foo$
```

You can see that there is a numbered list of output commands. To repeat a numbered command, you can use the bang character, `!`. `!<number>` will repeat the number command verbatim:

```
!10
```

The following is what you should see on running the preceding command:

```
ubuntu@commandlinebook:~/foo$ !10
cat numbers.txt | sort -n
1
1
3
5
19
25
ubuntu@commandlinebook:~/foo$
```

A double bang, `!!`, will repeat the last command.

You can also cycle through the list of commands with the up and down arrow keys on the keyboard.

You can perform a reverse command search by typing *Ctrl + R* at an empty command line. Then begin typing some substring of a command you'd like to search for. Bash will attempt to find a matching command somewhere in your history. If multiple commands match, the last one will be picked, but you can cycle through the others by pressing *Ctrl + R* repeatedly.

`cd -` will take you back to the last directory you came from, even if it's halfway across the system.

A thing that confuses some people is hitting *Ctrl + S*. This will stop all output to a terminal session, and it will appear as if your session is frozen. To unfreeze the session, simply press *Ctrl + Q*.

Getting help

There are a number of resources available, both built into the command line and also externally. One command that you will always find yourself using is the man command (short for manual page). For example, type in man man to read what the man command can do. You should see something similar to this:

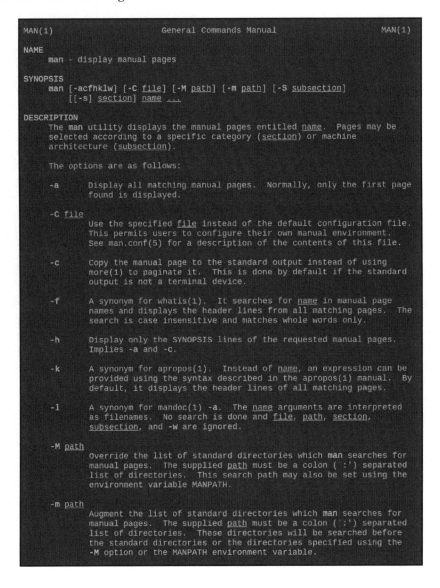

Chapter 2

Let's take a look at two options we use just about every day, `man -a` and `man -k`, as you will use them a lot for finding man pages at the command line. Go ahead and type `man -k .` in the command line to view all of the man pages that are installed on the system. If you are using the same Linux distribution as us, about 2,000 manuals just scrolled down your screen, that's a lot to read! We don't expect you to start from the top and read every one (feel free to do so if you're having trouble sleeping), so let's figure out some smarter ways to navigate all of these manuals.

If you wanted to slowly scroll through the entire list of manuals, you could run `man -k . | more` and just keep tapping the space bar to view the entire list. However, this is inefficient. Notice in the previous examples we were searching using a dot (.) instead of a string. Let's try this again, but this time remove the dot and enter a word:

```
man -k column
```

The following is what you should see on running the preceding command:

```
ubuntu@commandlinebook:~$ man -k column
col1 (1)            - awk and print a column (based on the name of the program, 1-9)
col2 (1)            - awk and print a column (based on the name of the program, 1-9)
col3 (1)            - awk and print a column (based on the name of the program, 1-9)
col4 (1)            - awk and print a column (based on the name of the program, 1-9)
col5 (1)            - awk and print a column (based on the name of the program, 1-9)
col6 (1)            - awk and print a column (based on the name of the program, 1-9)
col7 (1)            - awk and print a column (based on the name of the program, 1-9)
col8 (1)            - awk and print a column (based on the name of the program, 1-9)
col9 (1)            - awk and print a column (based on the name of the program, 1-9)
colrm (1)           - remove columns from a file
column (1)          - columnate lists
git-column (1)      - Display data in columns
NF (1)              - awk and print a column (based on the name of the program, 1-9)
Text::CharWidth (3pm) - Get number of occupied columns of a string on terminal
ubuntu@commandlinebook:~$
```

Much better! Now I can quickly see whether there's a man page for the column command instead of parsing through thousands of pages.

The manual is terrific, but sometimes it's not quite enough. Enter the Internet. Sites such as Stack Overflow and Stack Exchange can be invaluable when trying to figure out esoteric issues with commands, or give nice examples. The Internet is a big place: someone will be trying to do what you are doing and it's likely they had the same issues you're having. Answered questions might already exist with your exact issue, or you could submit a new question.

Customizing the shell

You might have noticed the prompt every time you enter a command to the left. Depending on your system, it might look a little different from mine. Let's fix that! For example, wouldn't it be great if you didn't have to type pwd all the time just to see where you are? Go ahead and enter the following:

```
export PS1="\u@\h:\w>"
```

You should see something like this:

```
ubuntu@commandlinebook:~$ pwd
/home/ubuntu
ubuntu@commandlinebook:~$
ubuntu@commandlinebook:~$
ubuntu@commandlinebook:~$ export PS1="\u@\h:\w>"
ubuntu@commandlinebook:~>
ubuntu@commandlinebook:~>pwd
/home/ubuntu
ubuntu@commandlinebook:~>
```

Pretty nifty, right? You can add that command inside your ~/.bash_profile file to keep it permanent. You can use any editor that you like (vim, nano, emacs) to open the file. For example, we used vim:

vim ~/.bash_profile

There's also an easy generator located at http://ezprompt.net/, which you can use to customize your bash prompt even further. Take a look!

Now that you understand the basics and totally tricked out your bash prompt, let's go ahead and work on an actual dataset!

Summary

As you can see, the command line is very powerful for everyday tasks. We learned how to do basic things, such as create files and directories, and navigate a system via the command line. We learned about manual pages, where to find help, and how to customize the shell.

In the next chapter, we'll take what you learned here and apply it against a real dataset. Feel free to come back to this chapter as it will be helpful throughout the rest of this book.

3
Shell Workflows, and Data Acquisition and Massaging

In this chapter, we're going to work on an actual dataset and do some basic analysis. We'll learn how to download files straight from the command line, determine what type of file it is, and parse the data using a number of commands. We'll also cover how to perform non-interactive detached processing and review some common terminal multiplexers that enable us to prettify the command line as well as organize detached processing.

In this chapter, we'll cover the following topics:

- How to download a dataset using the command line
- Using built-in tools to inspect the data and its type
- How to perform a word count in bash
- Analyzing a dataset with some simple commands
- Detached processing
- Terminal multiplexers

Download the data

Now that we have an understanding of the command line, let's do something cool with it! Say we had a couple datasets full of book reviews from Amazon, and we wanted to only view the reviews about Packt Publishing. First, let's go ahead and grab the data (if you are using the Docker container, the data is located in /data):

```
curl -O
https://s3.amazonaws.com/amazon-reviews-pds/tsv/amazon_reviews_us_Digital_E
book_Purchase_v1_00.tsv.gz && curl -O
https://s3.amazonaws.com/amazon-reviews-pds/tsv/amazon_reviews_us_Digital_E
book_Purchase_v1_01.tsv.gz
```

You should see the following:

We are introducing a couple of new commands and features here to download the files. First, we call the curl command to download the file. You can run curl --help to view all of the options available, or man curl, but we wanted to download a remote file and save it as the original filename, so we used the -O option. Second, notice the double ampersands (&&)? Since we want to download both files at the same time (with no errors), the double ampersand allows us to combine two commands together. If the first command fails, the second command won't run.

Now you might be asking yourself, "What if I want to run multiple commands and I don't care whether the first command fails, I want to it to run anyway!" Well, you're in luck! If you replace the double ampersands with a semicolon, ecoh "this isn't a command" ; echo "but this is", you should see the following:

Ubuntu comes with a nice little helper if you mistype a command and recommends what command you probably should have typed. If you're running this on another system, you might not see it, but you will see **ecoh: command not found**.

Using the file command

Once the data is done downloading, let's take a look and see what we've got. Go ahead and run `ls -al amazon*` to make sure the files actually downloaded:

```
ubuntu@commandlinebook:~>ls -al amazon*
-rw-rw-r-- 1 ubuntu ubuntu 2689739299 May 12 19:08 amazon_reviews_us_Digital_Ebook_Purchase_v1_00.tsv.gz
-rw-rw-r-- 1 ubuntu ubuntu 1294879074 May 12 19:08 amazon_reviews_us_Digital_Ebook_Purchase_v1_01.tsv.gz
ubuntu@commandlinebook:~>
```

If you have anything else in this directory named `amazon`, that will show up as well. Now that the files are downloaded, let's introduce a new command, called `file`. Go ahead and run the following `file amazon*` command:

```
ubuntu@commandlinebook:~>file amazon*
amazon_reviews_us_Digital_Ebook_Purchase_v1_00.tsv.gz: gzip compressed data, from FAT filesystem (MS-DOS, OS/2, NT)
amazon_reviews_us_Digital_Ebook_Purchase_v1_01.tsv.gz: gzip compressed data, from FAT filesystem (MS-DOS, OS/2, NT)
ubuntu@commandlinebook:~>
```

Wow, without any parameters set, the `file` command was able to figure out that this is a compressed archive. You'll use the `file` command a lot to determine the type of files you're working with. Let's decompress the files so we can work with them. This might take a little bit, depending on the speed of your system.

To do so, run the following:

```
zcat amazon_reviews_us_Digital_Ebook_Purchase_v1_00.tsv.gz >>
amazon_reviews_us_Digital_Ebook_Purchase_v1_00.tsv && zcat
amazon_reviews_us_Digital_Ebook_Purchase_v1_01.tsv.gz >>
amazon_reviews_us_Digital_Ebook_Purchase_v1_01.tsv
```

Shell Workflows, and Data Acquisition and Massaging

Go ahead and run the `file` command again against the new datasets. Notice anything different? Check out the following:

```
ubuntu@commandlinebook:~>file amazon_reviews_us_Digital_Ebook_Purchase_v1_0*
amazon_reviews_us_Digital_Ebook_Purchase_v1_00.tsv: UTF-8 Unicode text, with very long lines
amazon_reviews_us_Digital_Ebook_Purchase_v1_01.tsv: UTF-8 Unicode text, with very long lines
ubuntu@commandlinebook:~>
```

Very cool! The `file` command was able to verify that we are working with text files, and it seems like a lot of text **with very long lines**. Let's take a look and sample one of the datasets to see what we're working with. To do so, we can use the `more` command:

```
more amazon_reviews_us_Digital_Ebook_Purchase_v1_01.tsv
```

We'll just sample the first file we downloaded:

Very long lines indeed! You can keep hitting the spacebar to view the file (it might take you a while to read the entire thing) and if you want to exit, just hit the *Q* key. Don't forget to `man more` for more information on more.

[34]

Performing a word count

Now that we have some data to work with, let's combine the two files together into a single file. To do so, perform the following:

```
cat *.tsv > reviews.tsv
```

This is what you should see once you run the preceding command:

```
ubuntu@commandlinebook:~>cat *.tsv > reviews.tsv
ubuntu@commandlinebook:~>
```

Excellent. Let's say we wanted to count how many words or lines are in this file. Let's introduce the `wc` command. `wc` is short for (you guessed it) word count. Let's quickly `man wc` to see the options available:

```
WC(1)                            User Commands                           WC(1)

NAME
       wc - print newline, word, and byte counts for each file

SYNOPSIS
       wc [OPTION]... [FILE]...
       wc [OPTION]... --files0-from=F

DESCRIPTION
       Print  newline, word, and byte counts for each FILE, and a total line if more than one FILE is specified.  A word is a non-zero-length sequence of charac‐
       ters delimited by white space.

       With no FILE, or when FILE is -, read standard input.

       The options below may be used to select which counts are printed, always in the following order: newline, word, character, byte, maximum line length.

       -c, --bytes
              print the byte counts

       -m, --chars
              print the character counts

       -l, --lines
              print the newline counts

       --files0-from=F
              read input from the files specified by NUL-terminated names in file F; If F is - then read names from standard input

       -L, --max-line-length
              print the maximum display width

       -w, --words
              print the word counts

       --help display this help and exit

       --version
              output version information and exit

AUTHOR
       Written by Paul Rubin and David MacKenzie.

REPORTING BUGS
       GNU coreutils online help: <http://www.gnu.org/software/coreutils/>
       Report wc translation bugs to <http://translationproject.org/team/>

COPYRIGHT
       Copyright © 2016 Free Software Foundation, Inc.  License GPLv3+: GNU GPL version 3 or later <http://gnu.org/licenses/gpl.html>.
       This is free software: you are free to change and redistribute it.  There is NO WARRANTY, to the extent permitted by law.

SEE ALSO
 Manual page wc(1) line 1 (press h for help or q to quit)
```

Looks like wc can count the lines and also the words of a file. Let's see how many lines our file actually has:

```
wc -l reviews.tsv
```

The following is what you should see once you run the preceding command:

```
ubuntu@commandlinebook:~>wc -l reviews.tsv
17622417 reviews.tsv
ubuntu@commandlinebook:~>
```

That's a lot of lines! What about words? Run the following:

```
wc -w reviews.tsv
```

```
ubuntu@commandlinebook:~>wc -w reviews.tsv
1689661747 reviews.tsv
ubuntu@commandlinebook:~>
```

This looks like a great dataset to use. It's not big data by any means, but there's a lot of cool stuff we can do with it. For example, did you notice the header in the file from earlier? It's kind of hard to see since there's a lot of data being displayed on the screen. Let's strip just the headers out and see what we have:

```
head -n1 reviews.tsv
```

The following is what you should see once you run the preceding command:

```
ubuntu@commandlinebook:~>head -n1 reviews.tsv
marketplace    customer_id    review_id    product_id    product_parent  product_title  product_category    star_rating    helpful_votes    total_votes
ine    verified_purchase    review_headline review_body   review_date
ubuntu@commandlinebook:~>
```

Great, now we have a list of the headers we can use. Let's clean this up a bit. Imagine we're only interested in the `produce_title`, `star_rating`, `review_headline`, and `review_body` columns. Copying and pasting throughout the file would take hours, so let's introduce a new command called `cut`.

[36]

Chapter 3

Introduction to cut

Let's break the command down before you run it. The `cut` command removes sections from each line of a file. The `-d` parameter tells `cut` we are working with a **tsv (tab separated values)**, and the `-f` parameter tells `cut` what fields we are interested in. Since `product_title` is the sixth field in our file, we started with that:

```
cut -d$'\t' -f 6,8,13,14 reviews.tsv | more
```

 Unlike most programs, cut starts at 1 instead of 0.

Let's see the results:

Shell Workflows, and Data Acquisition and Massaging

Much better! Let's go ahead and save this as a new file:

```
cut -d$'\t' -f 6,8,13,14 reviews.tsv > stripped_reviews.tsv
```

The following is what you should see once you run the preceding command:

```
ubuntu@commandlinebook:~>cut -d$'\t' -f 6,8,13,14 reviews.tsv > stripped_reviews.tsv
ubuntu@commandlinebook:~>
```

Let's see how many times the word `Packt` shows up in this dataset:

```
grep -i Packt stripped_reviews.tsv | wc -w
```

The following is what you should see once you run the preceding command:

```
ubuntu@commandlinebook:~>grep -i packt stripped_reviews.tsv | wc -w
140197
ubuntu@commandlinebook:~>
```

Let's convert this from `.tsv` to `.csv` so we have a little more structure to work with:

```
cat stripped_reviews.tsv | tr "\\t" "," > all_reviews.csv
```

The following is what you should see once you run the preceding command:

```
ubuntu@commandlinebook:~>cat stripped_reviews.tsv | tr "\\t" "," > all_reviews.csv
ubuntu@commandlinebook:~>
```

Now let's go ahead and filter out all of the reviews that have the word `Packt` in them:

```
cat all_reviews.csv | awk -F "," '{print $4}' | grep -i Packt
```

The following is what you should see once you run the preceding command:

```
ubuntu@commandlinebook:~$ cat all_reviews.csv | awk -F "," '{print $4}' | grep -i Packt
```

[terminal output of reviews mentioning Packt]

Interesting! Using the commands you just learned, go ahead and play with this dataset for a bit.

We will talk more about the `tr` command in Chapter 5, *Loops, Functions, and String Processing*; for now, don't worry about it.

Detached processing

Detached processing runs a command in the background. This means that terminal control is immediately returned to the shell process while the detached process runs in the background. With job control, these back grounded processes can be resumed in the foreground or killed directly.

How to background a process

Remember when we used the double ampersand to conditionally execute two commands that run one after another? By using a single ampersand, you can fork a process in the background and let it run. Let's use the command to save to a new file and run in the background:

```
cat all_reviews.csv | awk -F "," '{print $4}' | grep -i Packt > background_words.txt &
```

This will take the example from earlier but run it in the background, like so:

```
ubuntu@commandlinebook:~>cat all_reviews.csv | awk -F "," '{print $4}' | grep -i Packt > background_words.txt &
[1] 1504
ubuntu@commandlinebook:~>
```

Notice to `<output> [1] 1504</output>` that was printed (avoiding all the output!) this shows you that the job was run successfully in the background. You can run `tail -F background_words.txt` to view the data in real time as it runs in the background:

```
ubuntu@commandlinebook:~>cat all_reviews.csv | awk -F "," '{print $4}' | grep -i Packt > background_words.txt &
[1] 1504
ubuntu@commandlinebook:~>tail -f background_words.txt
Breits nach den ersten Zeilen der Leseprobe musste ich mehr erfahren. Das Buch Revue des Todes\\" hat mich gepackt und bewegt.<br />Die bildhafte Sprache von Bärbel Upker lässt reale Bilder beim Lesen entstehen
Da mich die beiden erste beiden Gesichten der Reihe Das Doktorhaus am See\\" gepackt haben
[[ASIN:1849601924 Unreal Development Kit Game Programming with UnrealScript: Beginner's Guide]]<br /><br />I purchased this book through the Packt Publishing website
I must say the title should be \\"Unrealscript for Dummies\\". It was written in a manner for a non-programmer to understand.<br /><br />I highly recommend you to rchase this book if you want to learn Unrealscript.
Als ehemaliger Lastwagenchauffeur konnte ich mich sehr gut mit der Hauptperson identifizieren. Auch die Geschichte selbst hat mich sofort gepackt. Ich konnte nicht ders
I was very disappointed after I read 20% of this book that there are numerous missing and erroneous paragraphs with important facts or illustrations missing. This on y pertains to the Kindle edition as all these sections are correct as per PDF from Packt's own website. I bought the Kindle version due to PDF rendering issues for Kindle. This is not a good reflection on Kindle edition or Amazon. e.g look at the section on \\"install\\" in Chapter 3 (should be page 43) - the example bundles fter the \\"lb\\" command has the bundle with ID 7 missing from Kindle edition
I was waiting for many years for a serious book around Cakephp framework. And finally it came from Packt Ed and his author Mariano Iglesias.<br />I enjoy all the top
This book was horrible. Thank goodness I purchased the Kindle version for half the price of the printed book. This book is supposed to help developers new to NetBe ns learn how to develope application using the Netbeans Platform. Unfortunately the author leaves out details in how to perform some of the tasks he tells you to do and then the code examples are littered with errors making it pointless to copy and paste the code and try to figure your way through the sample. I even obtained the updated source code from Packt Publishing and it was missing some of the modules needed to make the application work completely. I was given the option to run the a plication without enabling the features of the missing modules. I chose to do that and everything was in German. Fortunately I can read German
Unterhaltsam verpacktes Wissen
Interessante und naturwissentschaftliche Erkenntnisse toll verpackt mit einer spannenden Geschichte. Dieckmanns werk liegt voll im Trend der \\"FactFiction\\" wie ic es nennen würde. Wer gerne Werke wie die von Hawkings und Co. liest
Der Autor erklärt das aktuelle Wissen über die Zusammenhänge der Welt (Evolution: warum - wohin - sind wir allein im All - u.s.w.) verpackt in eine spannende Geschic
```

To bring the job back from the **bg (background)**, type `fg` and you brought the process back to the foreground like so:

```
ubuntu@commandlinebook:~>fg
cat all_reviews.csv | awk -F "," '{print $4}' | grep -i Packt > background_words.txt
```

Go ahead and run a couple of commands in the background. You can use the `jobs` command to view them all. Feel free to check the manual page for the `jobs` command by entering `man jobs` for more options.

Disregarding SIGHUP

Commands are attached to their controlling command-line terminal by default. When the command line terminates, child processes (backgrounded or not) are sent a SIGHUP and should terminate. Let's say you wanted to run a command and keep it running if you log out. `nohup` comes in handy, especially if you're working on remote systems and have a need to log out, or you're worried about your connection to the server that keeps disconnecting (I'm looking at you, Amtrak WiFi).

Go ahead and run the command we ran earlier, but add `nohup` to the beginning, like so:

```
nohup cat all_reviews.csv | awk -F "," '{print $4}' | grep -i Packt > background_words.txt &
```

Now, log out of your shell by typing `logout` or by using `control-d`, and then bring the shell back up and run `tail -f background_words.txt`. You'll notice that the command is still running in the background and the file is being updated. You might have tried to bring the command back by issuing `fg` and noticed it didn't work. Keep that in mind as `nohup` the command will run until completion or failure or until you `kill` the process. Feel free to check out the manual page for `kill` by doing a `man kill`, as there's a lot of options to choose from.

Terminal multiplexers

Let's now take a look at the `screen` command, it will give you the ability to do many different things, as we will see in the following section.

Introduction to screen

So far, you've learned how to run a command in the background and you've mastered `nohup`. Now it's time to talk about the `screen` command. `screen` gives you the ability to attach and detach sessions on the fly, keep a shell active even with network disruptions, disconnect and reconnect to a shell from multiple locations, share a shell with a remote user, and keep a long-running process running without maintaining an active session.

Shell Workflows, and Data Acquisition and Massaging

First, let's make sure you have `screen` and `tmux` (we will use `tmux` later) installed. In Ubuntu, run the following:

```
sudo apt install -y screen tmux
```

You might already have it installed (depending on which version of Ubuntu you are running), but better safe than sorry. Now, let's go ahead and fire up `screen`:

```
screen
```

You should see the following:

```
Screen version 4.03.01 (GNU) 28-Jun-15

Copyright (c) 2010 Juergen Weigert, Sadrul Habib Chowdhury
Copyright (c) 2008, 2009 Juergen Weigert, Michael Schroeder, Micah Cowan, Sadrul Habib Chowdhury
Copyright (c) 1993-2002, 2003, 2005, 2006, 2007 Juergen Weigert, Michael Schroeder
Copyright (c) 1987 Oliver Laumann

This program is free software; you can redistribute it and/or modify it under the terms of the GNU General Public License as published by the Free Software
Foundation; either version 3, or (at your option) any later version.

This program is distributed in the hope that it will be useful, but WITHOUT ANY WARRANTY; without even the implied warranty of MERCHANTABILITY or FITNESS FOR A
PARTICULAR PURPOSE. See the GNU General Public License for more details.

You should have received a copy of the GNU General Public License along with this program (see the file COPYING); if not, see http://www.gnu.org/licenses/, or
contact Free Software Foundation, Inc., 51 Franklin Street, Fifth Floor, Boston, MA 02111-1301 USA.

Send bugreports, fixes, enhancements, t-shirts, money, beer & pizza to screen-devel@gnu.org

Capabilities:
+copy +remote-detach +power-detach +multi-attach +multi-user +font +color-256 +utf8 +rxvt +builtin-telnet
```

Go ahead and send the team some pizza and beer (really, these folks are great!) and hit the spacebar to continue. You'll notice... well, nothing really changed. The command prompt is still the same, just some information about copyrights and where to send beer money appeared. Let's go ahead and run a new command, called `top`. The top command (table of processes) shows you all of the processes that are currently running. Go ahead and give it a try!

Your output will look slightly different.

Execute the `top`:

```
top
```

With `top` running:

```
top - 19:51:06 up 43 min,  2 users,  load average: 0.00, 0.02, 0.08
Tasks: 133 total,   1 running, 132 sleeping,   0 stopped,   0 zombie
%Cpu(s):  0.0 us,  0.0 sy,  0.0 ni,100.0 id,  0.0 wa,  0.0 hi,  0.0 si,  0.0 st
KiB Mem : 16431384 total,  8011860 free,    82164 used,  8337360 buff/cache
KiB Swap:        0 total,        0 free,        0 used. 16051560 avail Mem

  PID USER      PR  NI    VIRT    RES    SHR S  %CPU %MEM     TIME+ COMMAND
    1 root      20   0   37844   5856   3980 S   0.0  0.0   0:02.45 systemd
    2 root      20   0       0      0      0 S   0.0  0.0   0:00.00 kthreadd
    3 root      20   0       0      0      0 S   0.0  0.0   0:00.00 ksoftirqd/0
    5 root       0 -20       0      0      0 S   0.0  0.0   0:00.00 kworker/0:0H
    7 root      20   0       0      0      0 S   0.0  0.0   0:00.02 rcu_sched
    8 root      20   0       0      0      0 S   0.0  0.0   0:00.00 rcu_bh
    9 root      rt   0       0      0      0 S   0.0  0.0   0:00.00 migration/0
   10 root      rt   0       0      0      0 S   0.0  0.0   0:00.01 watchdog/0
   11 root      rt   0       0      0      0 S   0.0  0.0   0:00.00 watchdog/1
   12 root      rt   0       0      0      0 S   0.0  0.0   0:00.00 migration/1
   13 root      20   0       0      0      0 S   0.0  0.0   0:00.01 ksoftirqd/1
   15 root       0 -20       0      0      0 S   0.0  0.0   0:00.00 kworker/1:0H
   16 root      rt   0       0      0      0 S   0.0  0.0   0:00.00 watchdog/2
   17 root      rt   0       0      0      0 S   0.0  0.0   0:00.00 migration/2
   18 root      20   0       0      0      0 S   0.0  0.0   0:00.00 ksoftirqd/2
   20 root       0 -20       0      0      0 S   0.0  0.0   0:00.00 kworker/2:0H
   21 root      rt   0       0      0      0 S   0.0  0.0   0:00.00 watchdog/3
   22 root      rt   0       0      0      0 S   0.0  0.0   0:00.00 migration/3
   23 root      20   0       0      0      0 S   0.0  0.0   0:00.00 ksoftirqd/3
   25 root       0 -20       0      0      0 S   0.0  0.0   0:00.00 kworker/3:0H
   26 root      20   0       0      0      0 S   0.0  0.0   0:00.00 kdevtmpfs
   27 root       0 -20       0      0      0 S   0.0  0.0   0:00.00 netns
   28 root       0 -20       0      0      0 S   0.0  0.0   0:00.00 perf
   29 root      20   0       0      0      0 S   0.0  0.0   0:00.00 xenwatch
   30 root      20   0       0      0      0 S   0.0  0.0   0:00.00 xenbus
   32 root      20   0       0      0      0 S   0.0  0.0   0:00.00 khungtaskd
   33 root       0 -20       0      0      0 S   0.0  0.0   0:00.00 writeback
   34 root      25   5       0      0      0 S   0.0  0.0   0:00.00 ksmd
   35 root      39  19       0      0      0 S   0.0  0.0   0:00.00 khugepaged
   36 root       0 -20       0      0      0 S   0.0  0.0   0:00.00 crypto
   37 root       0 -20       0      0      0 S   0.0  0.0   0:00.00 kintegrityd
   38 root       0 -20       0      0      0 S   0.0  0.0   0:00.00 bioset
   39 root       0 -20       0      0      0 S   0.0  0.0   0:00.00 kblockd
   40 root       0 -20       0      0      0 S   0.0  0.0   0:00.00 ata_sff
   41 root       0 -20       0      0      0 S   0.0  0.0   0:00.00 md
   42 root       0 -20       0      0      0 S   0.0  0.0   0:00.00 devfreq_wq
   43 root      20   0       0      0      0 S   0.0  0.0   0:00.00 kworker/1:1
   44 root      20   0       0      0      0 S   0.0  0.0   0:00.02 kworker/2:1
   48 root      20   0       0      0      0 S   0.0  0.0   0:00.00 kswapd0
   49 root       0 -20       0      0      0 S   0.0  0.0   0:00.00 vmstat
   50 root      20   0       0      0      0 S   0.0  0.0   0:00.00 fsnotify_mark
   51 root      20   0       0      0      0 S   0.0  0.0   0:00.00 ecryptfs-kthrea
   67 root       0 -20       0      0      0 S   0.0  0.0   0:00.00 kthrotld
   68 root       0 -20       0      0      0 S   0.0  0.0   0:00.00 bioset
   69 root       0 -20       0      0      0 S   0.0  0.0   0:00.00 bioset
```

Admire the awesomeness of `top`. This is a great command to use if you ever what to know what's taking up a lot of the system's resources.

While `top` is running, let's go ahead and detach from `screen`. Type the following:

```
<key>Ctrl+a</key> d
```

Notice that the screen went back to a clean shell:

```
[detached from 1788.pts-1.commandlinebook]
ubuntu@commandlinebook:~>
```

To check whether the `screen` session is still active, let's go ahead and run `screen -r`. Notice that the `top` command didn't die—it ran in a screen session. What's great is that you can log out of this session, reconnect, and attach the `screen` session like nothing happened. It's very useful for running long processes from a laptop or any place where you'll need to disconnect for a bit.

Go ahead and run multiple `screen` sessions. You can view them by running `screen -list`.

Sharing a screen session between multiple users

We've all been there: trying to troubleshoot someone's code remotely when you're unable to see what's going on is a very painful process. A user can create a shared session by doing the following:

```
screen -d -m -S shared_screen
```

And while you're logged into the same machine, go ahead and type the following:

```
screen -x shared_screen
```

Introduction to tmux

`tmux` is the newest terminal multiplexer on the block, with a lot of great features to enhance your command line skills and provides a lot of features over just the standard shell. Let's fire it up and check it out:

```
tmux
```

You should see something like this when you run `tmux`:

Output for tmux command

Chapter 3

One thing to keep in mind is that, by default, all `tmux` commands require the prefix *Ctrl + B* before you can run `tmux` commands. For example, let's try a couple out. Having one shell window is great, but how about two?

Output for tmux command with two shells

How about two more but on the bottom?

```
<key>Ctrl+b</key> "
<key>Ctrl+b</key> <key></key>
<key>Ctrl+b</key> "
```

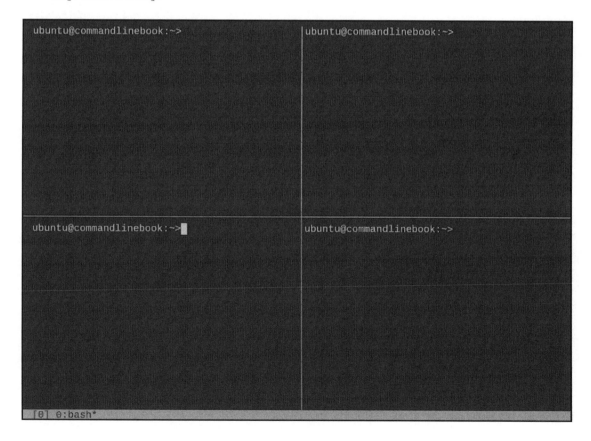

Pretty awesome, right? Go ahead and customize your `tmux` session to your liking. There's a bunch of options located in the `man` page, `man tmux`, to choose from. Our personal favorites are `<key>Ctrl+b</key> : setw synchronize-panes on <key>enter</key>`. Now, go ahead and type `top`. Did you notice that all of the panes are the same? This comes in handy when you're logged into multiple servers and need to run a command across them all manually.

Summary

In this chapter, we only scratched the surface on what we can do with the command line. We were able to download a dataset, save it, inspect the file type, and perform some simple analytics. The word count example is considered the "Hello, World" of data science and we saw just how easy it is to perform in bash.

We then took your shell customization to the next level by using terminal multiplexers and background processes. Think of it like using an IDE, but for the command line. It will make working with bash a lot easier.

Being able to control processes and workflows will improve productivity. Detached processing ensures programs can complete without interruption. The terminal multiplexer provides a means of maximizing the use of screen real-estate, while also providing a detached processing environment, which is a double win for all.

In the next chapter, we'll explore reusable shell bash scripts and functions.

4
Bash Functions and Data Visualization

So far, we've been working with bash interactively and had to rely on the bash `history` for what we've done. Wouldn't it be nice if you had a portable way to share and store the commands you want to run? Well, that functionality exists in the form of shell scripts composed of shell functions.

We're going to extend the history we covered in Chapter 1, *Data Science at the Command Line and Setting It Up*. Terminals originated as text-only devices and evolved graphical support for simple drawing primitives, such as rendering enclosed cells in tabular data. The pinnacle of Terminal graphics was made by DEC with canvas and vector-graphic support in the form of SIXEL and REGIS graphics, respectively. As physical Terminals became a thing of the past, lightweight Terminal emulators regressed to being text-only. A renaissance in graphics support from Terminal emulators has been occurring with the alacritty, wsltty, xterm, mlterm, st, iTerm2, and hterm emulators.

We recommend wsltty with SIXEL support for Windows users, xterm or mlterm with SIXEL support for Linux users, and iTerm2 on macOS with PNG rendering (SIXEL support may be added in the future).

With a recommended Terminal emulator, we will show off canvas-style graphical rendering in the Terminal, and of course, include text mode support for DUMB Terminals. We'll only mention that ascii-art libraries exists, `aalib` (**ascii art lib**), `libcaca`, and braille fonts that attempt to render graphics to the Terminal using font characters only. Here, we'll work with SIXEL for Linux/Windows and PNG for macOS, and leave DUMB Terminal output for all advanced alternatives as an adventure for the reader. In this chapter, we'll cover the following topics:

- How to execute a script
- Function arguments/parameters

- Advanced shell scripting
- How to configure your Terminal for graphics mode
- Data mining graphable data
- Graphing data with gnuplot

My first shell script

Our first shell script will cover the basics of how to tell the computer to run the shell script.

She bangs, she bangs!

We're not talking about that popular Ricky Martin song. We're talking about what every bash script needs in order to run. If you've worked with other programming languages, you may have noticed the first line always starts with a `#!`. This tells the system which interpreter to use. For example, if you've worked with Python before, you've probably seen `#!/usr/bin/env python2.7` in a script. With bash, it's no different. Let's go ahead and create a new file named `hello_world.sh` and enter the following:

```
#!/bin/bash
# A function to greet everyone
greet_everyone() {
  echo Hello, World!
}
greet_yourself() {
  echo Hello, ${USER}
}
greet_everyone
greet_yourself
```

 File editors are the new, hip thing to debate about on the Internet. For example, search for `vim` versus `emacs` or `nano` versus `pico`. If you don't have a favorite editor, we won't force your selection, but you should use a Very Immensely Method to find your one true editor.

Go ahead and save this file as `hello_world.sh` and then let's make the script executable:

```
chmod +x hello_world.sh
```

Now, you can run the script like so:

```
./hello_world.sh
```

Let's break this down. The first line is the shebang that we mentioned. Our functions are called `greet_everyone` and `greet_yourself`. Inside the curly brackets, { }, we can run as many commands as we want. Finally, the functions are called below it. Also, notice the `${USER}` variable inside the script. You might be wondering how bash was smart enough to print out your username without you defining it. Every bash environment has a set of preconfigured variables that you can view. Go ahead and run the `printenv` command to see what's available.

This is great if we want to greet the entire world and use your username. But, what if we want to take this further?

Function arguments, positional parameters, and IFS

Functional arguments, positional parameters, and the **IFS (internal field separator)** are advanced list-processing mechanics in bash. We'll cover each of them in turn to ensure a base knowledge of how the shell interacts with them.

Prompt me baby one more time

We discussed how to invoke our function, but how do we prompt our users for input? The computer can't read your mind—it can only read your keyboard input! For bash to read input, you'll have to use the (you guessed it) `read` command. Let's expand our function's capabilities. Go ahead and modify your `hello_world.sh` script from the previous section with the following:

```
#!/bin/bash
# A function to greet everyone
echo Who would you like to greet?
read name
greet_yourself() {
  echo Hello, ${1:-$USER}!
}
greet_yourself $name
```

Bash Functions and Data Visualization

We've added the `read name` code, replaced the `${USER}` variable with `${1:-$USER}` in the `greet_yourself` function, and added our first argument to our `greet_yourself $name` function call. When `$name` is passed into the `greet_yourself` function, it's assigned to the `$1` variable. That `${1:-$USER}` magic variable is saying expand `$1`; if empty, replace with `$USER` retaining the same output behavior of our original function if no username is provided by just pressing the `enter` key. Run it again to see the following:

```
ubuntu@commandlinebook:~$ ./hello_world.sh
Who would you like to greet?
Thor
Hello, Thor!
ubuntu@commandlinebook:~$
```

Let's focus on just our function. Paste the following code into your shell:

```
<<EOF cat >greetlib.sh
greet_yourself() {
   echo Hello, \${1:-\$USER}!
}
EOF
```

This is a fancy means of creating the `greetlib.sh` file. The `<<EOF` here is doc redirection that indicates that we want to specify the standard input to `cat` and redirect its standard output to `greetlib.sh`. Everything after that first line is shell-interpreted content that's to be concatenated to the end of our output file until `EOF` is read. Shell-interpreted content means that variables are replaced with values from your current shell environment, we've escaped our shell variables with `\$` so that they will be rendered into the `greetlib.sh` file as `$` and not interpreted into actual values. Finally, we can source our function into our current shell environment and invoke it. We'll practice that in the next section.

Feed the function input!

Our shell function accepts arguments, known as positional parameters, which are the equivalent of ARGV from a POSIX C runtime. Function arguments are automatically assigned by their numeric position to variables in this form: $1, $2, $3, .., $9. The $0 variable exists, but contains the name that was used to invoke the shell. Some inquiring minds might wonder what happens after the ninth argument. Well we need to use the full variable dereferencing syntax, for the tenth and eleventh variables, ${10} and ${11}, respectively. So what does that all look like? Check it out:

```
greet_yourself() {
  echo Hello, ${1:-$USER}!
}
. ./greetlib.sh
greet_yourself "Joey"
```

The . operator is used to read and evaluate a shell script in your current execution environment, as though you had typed all of greetlib.sh into the command line and pressed the enter key. This calls the greet_yourself function with the first positional parameter, "Joey", assigned to $1. To jump ahead, we have types of positional parameters: options (covered at the end of the chapter) and arguments. Options come in short and long forms and are identified by a single hyphen or double-hyphen, respectively. Short options are single characters and long options are full semantic words that describe values to set. If an argument needs a literal hyphen at the start of its value, it needs to be distinguished from options by proceeding with a double-hyphen. Hypothetically, this is gobbledygook looks like this:

```
greet_yourself --capitalize --name="Joey"
greet_yourself --lowercase -- -RoBoT1
```

These examples showcase how options and arguments can be passed to a function, because the options are just positional parameters. In the first greeting call, we assign --capitalize to the first positional parameter, $1, and --name="Joey" to the second positional parameter, $2. In the second greeting call, we assign --lowercase to $1, -- to $2, and -RoBoT1 to $3. Our function is basic and lacks the ability to process the --capitalize and --lowercase options as function features. We pretend the first greeting call should output "JOEY", and the second greeting -robot1. Some may wonder how a command can distinguish options that begin with a hyphen from an argument, such as -RoBoT1. The bare double-hyphen -- indicates that all following positional parameters are to be treated as arguments and not processed as options. Again, we'll dig into option processing at the end of the chapter, but it's easiest to show function invocations all at once.

Down the rabbit hole of IFS and bash arrays

Positional parameters are created from the arguments to a shell script, function, or the `set` command. The assignment of words to positional variables is accomplished by splitting the unquoted string along any of the delimiters contained within the IFS variable. The IFS variable defaults to the string, which consists of a space, tab, and newline characters. Since the IFS is a variable, it's possible to modify this variable, which is useful when iterating over non-space-delimited text:

```
IFS=:
for P in $PATH ; do
 echo $P
done
unset IFS
```

The preceding code exemplifies how the PATH variable, which consists minimally of `/bin:/usr/bin`, can be split with a colon delimiter so that each path segment can be manipulated. We expect the reader can extrapolate how this might be useful for iterating over comma-separated lists, or similar simply delimited datasets.

Due to limitations in modifying positional parameters, bash 4 introduced arrays. In the event that your shell scripts become sufficiently complex to require arrays, we encourage you to consider upgrading to a full-fledged scripting language, such as Perl, Python, or Ruby, that's better-suited to handling various list iterations that bash doesn't natively support. Delving in, bash arrays are zero-indexed, and are accessed with the `${ARRAY[#]}` special syntax, where the # sign should be replaced by the integer array index or the special values of @ or *, which represent the quoted elements or unquoted elements converted into a string. Here's some code as an example of bash arrays:

```
TMP_PATH=/bin:/usr/bin:/sbin:/usr/sbin
IFS=:
PATH_ARRAY=($TMP_PATH)
unset IFS
echo First element - ${PATH_ARRAY}
echo First element - ${PATH_ARRAY[0]}
echo Second element - ${PATH_ARRAY[1]}
echo All elements - ${PATH_ARRAY[*]}
echo All elements - ${PATH_ARRAY[@]}
```

Advanced shell scripting magic

This is the dark magic section of the chapter. It will demonstrate advanced shell scripting by taking the preceding lessons and features, and converting them into what could be considered a small program.

Here be dragons, ye be warned

A simple piece of introductory code is great to get a feel for the flavor of a language, but we're going to introduce some dark magic in the form of some complex utility functions that can be helpful in everyday situations. We'll use a `lineinfile` function to insert arbitrary text into a file—it's not a full-featured application, just enough to help ensure some simple text is injected into a file. The second function, `ncz`, leverages bash IP networking (yes, bash4 can support IP networking YMMV with your distro) to perform a socket test equivalent to what `netcat -z` does. Additionally, it shows how to make a function behave like a command-line program by parsing simple argument flags.

Text injection of text files

We're going to create a function that can inject text into an existing file. Here's our function:

```
lineinfile() {
 FILE=$1 ; shift
 LINE="^$1$" ; shift
 CONTEXT="$1.*" ; shift
 MODE=${1:-add} ; shift
 case "${MODE}" in
  add)
    grep -s "${LINE}" "${FILE}" || sed -i -e "s/\(${CONTEXT}\)/\1\n${LINE}/" "${FILE}"
    ;;
  del)
    grep -s "${LINE}" "${FILE}" || sed -i -e "/${LINE}/d" "${FILE}"
    ;;
 esac
}
```

The intended usage is as follows:

```
lineinfile <filename> <string> <insert-after-context-string> <add | [del]>
```

lineinfile starts off with the standard function() {} definition template. It reads the first positional parameter passed to the function, $1, into the FILE variable, and shifts the positional parameters so that each parameter's index is decremented by one, so $2 becomes $1, $3 becomes $2, and so on. The second parameter is assigned to the LINE variable and we prefix it with the regular expression start of line ^ and end of line $ delimiters to indicate that the string being injected must match an entire line (sorry, there's no advanced regex support in this simple function). The third parameter looks for context so that we can inject the line after the context. Again no ability to specify injecting before the context, just after the context if it exists. The fourth parameter is the operating mode of our lineinfile function to either add (adding text is the default behavior) or to delete (use the del mode).

Bash networks for fun and profit!

Sometimes, we need to interact with network services or APIs. Here, we'll introduce some complete code that tests TCP endpoints, which is useful for checking whether an API service is listening and available. This code can be pasted into your Terminal, or saved to a file and loaded into your shell environment with the . operator:

```
ncz() {
  OPTIND=1 ; while getopts ":hv" opt; do
   case ${opt} in
    v) VERBOSE=true
     ;;
    h|\?) printf "Usage: $0 [-v] <host | host:port>" ; return
     ;;
   esac
  done
  shift $(($OPTIND - 1))
  HOST=${1%:*}
  PORT=${1#*:}
  PORT=${2:-$PORT}
  (exec 6<>/dev/tcp/${HOST}/${PORT} 2>&1)
  RC=$?
  case "${VERBOSE}${RC}" in
   true0) printf "open\n";;
   true*) printf "closed\n";;
  esac
  return $RC
}
```

Now, this code has some minor magic. `getopts` is a function that parses positional parameters, according to POSIX processing into options, and assigns the next option to the variable specified, in this case opt. It supports short and long options, and options can have parameters; parameters would be stored in OPTARG. This example uses a trivial option string of `:hv`. The colon character indicates that invalid option flags should be denoted with the question mark character, `?`. The h option is for our help flag and v is used so we can set a VERBOSE flag. The `while` loop calls the `getopts` function, which modifies the positional parameters. When the `getopts` function completes, it's necessary to shift the processed positional parameters out so that we can treat non-options as function arguments. OPTIND is the index of the last option parsed, so subtracting one from that and shifting the positional parameters by that amount ensures that we only proper arguments remain in our positional parameters.

The code attempts to support accepting arguments in the form of `host:port` or `host port`. The support for single-parameter or two-parameter arguments is handled by always using the second argument as the port, and if there's no second argument, defaults to splitting the first parameter on the colon character using prefix and suffix removal. The `HOST=${1%:*}` assignment attempts to extract a host component from a `host:port` argument by expanding the first positional argument, stripping all trailing characters (`%` is a reverse-substitution match) to the first colon character (the delimiter between `host:port`) so that we're left with just the host portion of the variable. If the reverse match fails, which indicates no port components, the unmodified expansion of `$1` will be assigned. To get the port, we look at the second argument. If it doesn't exist, we default to the port extracted from the first positional argument by stripping the `host:` portion of `$1`.

The real dark magic involves file descriptors and bash's IP network support. We open file descriptor 6 inside a subshell. We attach the input/output of the socket created by `/dev/tcp/$HOST/$PORT` to this file descriptor. Anything written to the file descriptor will be sent via a TCP socket to `tcp://$HOST:$PORT`, and any responses can be read from the same file descriptor. As network connections can error, we capture the return code of the socket open to the RC (that's short for return code) variable. We then evaluate whether output is desired from a verbose option flag and the status of the return code, printing success/failure according to the return code. In C programs, a return code of 0 indicates success, so `true0` indicates that the function has invoked to request the verbose mode and a successful socket connection was made. Finally, the return code is returned from the function so that the status of the remote socket can be evaluated via a shell pipeline.

Here's a self-explanatory invocation of the preceding explanation:

```
ncz google.com:80 && echo "yay!! Interwebz are up!" || echo "booh! No kitties for us!"
```

From dumb Terminal to glam Terminal

We're going to use gnuplot to render dumb text graphics and canvas-style plots inside our Terminal. To begin, we need some basic configuration for our gnuplot startup. Put the following in `~/.gnuplot`:

```
set term dumb
```

Next, we need a wrapper around gnuplot to get some fancy graphical output. This wrapper looks at the GNUTERM environment variable of your current shell and does some calculations on the Terminal's width and height so that gnuplot knows how big a window it has. The wrapper will update our `~/.gnuplot` configuration with the graphics capabilities specified for our Terminal. We aren't going to delve into the wrapper, but just use it as another command. Here it is:

```
__gnuplot() {
 SIZE=$(stty size 2>/dev/null)
 SIZE=${SIZE:-$(tput lines) $(tput cols)}
 COLS=${SIZE#* }
 ROWS=${SIZE% *}
 XPX=${XPX:-13}
 YPX=${YPX:-24}
 COLUMNS=${COLUMNS:-${COLS}}
 LINES=$((${LINES:-${ROWS}}-3))
 case "${GNUTERM%% *}" in
 dumb) X=${COLUMNS} ; Y=${LINES} ; DCS_GUARD="cat" ;;
 png) X=$((XPX*COLUMNS)) ; Y=$((YPX*LINES)) ; DCS_GUARD="imgcat";;
 sixelgd) X=$((XPX*COLUMNS)) ; Y=$((YPX*LINES));;
 esac
 sed -i "s/^set term[[:space:]][^[:space:]]*/set term ${GNUTERM%% *}/" ~/.gnuplot
 GNUTERM="${GNUTERM} size $X,$Y" \gnuplot "$@" | ${DCS_GUARD:-cat}
}
alias barchart="FUNCNAME=barchart __barchart"
__barchart() {
 local STACKED
 local DATA
 OPTIND=1 ; while getopts ":hf:s" opt; do
 case ${opt} in
```

```
      f) [ -r "${OPTARG}" ] && DATA=$(printf '$data <<EOD\n' ; cat "${OPTARG}" ;
printf 'EOD\n')
      ;;
      s) STACKED="; set style histogram rowstacked ; set boxwidth 0.75"
      ;;
      h|\?) printf "Usage: ${FUNCNAME} [-s] [-f <file>] <gnuplot commands\n"
      return
      ;;
    esac
  done
  shift $(($OPTIND - 1))
  {
  cat <<-EOF
  $DATA
  set key autotitle columnheader outside
  set style data histograms ${STACKED}
  set style fill solid border lt -1
  set xtics rotate by -45
  EOF
  printf "%s" "$@"
  } | gnuplot
}
```

Depending on your OS and Terminal, you'll need to specify the correct graphics backend for your Terminal.

Windows users with wsltty, and Linux users with mlterm or xterm, should set the following environment variable:

```
export GNUTERM=sixelgd
```

macOS users with iTerm2 should use this environment variable:

```
export GNUTERM=png
```

Let's verify that we're able to plot a graphical test pattern. If your dumb Terminal doesn't support graphical mode, we include a text mode test afterwards.

For the graphical test, run the following:

```
gnuplot -e "set terminal $GNUTERM background rgb 'white'; test"
```

Bash Functions and Data Visualization

This should result in a graphical Terminal output like this:

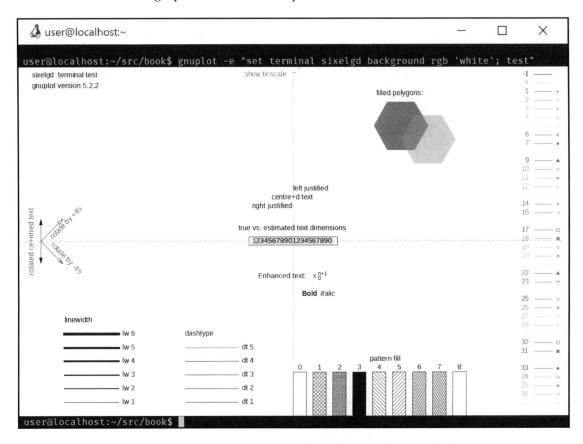

Some quick callouts to the test output are important for styling your output graphs. The line type on the far right of the test graphic is abbreviated as `lt` and provides the visual marker for the plotted tics (or points) of the plot, for example, *, +, and x. The linewidth, abbreviated to `lw`, is on the bottom left and sets the line's thickness for the plotted line.

If your Terminal doesn't support graphics mode, text plotting can be used. Invoke the text test:

```
GNUTERM=dumb \gnuplot
gnuplot> test
gnuplot> exit
```

Which should result in a Terminal output like this:

```
+-dumb  terminal test------------------show ticscale--XXXXX----------1-+---+--+
|                                $$$             XXXXXX              0 +...+ .|
| ^nuplot versi.> 5.2.2           :               XXXXXXXXX          1 ***** A|
| |        ..                        left justifiXXXXXXXXXX          2 ##### B|
| |         ..                    centre+d text   XXXXXXXXXX         3 $$$$$ C|
| |          ..           right justified:         XXXXXXXXXXX       4 %%%%% D|
| |           ..                       :             XXXXXXXXXX      5 @@@@@ E|
| |            ..                      :                XXXXXXX      6 &&&&& F|
| |..                 true vs. estimated text dimensions XXXXX       7 ===== G|
+.cannot rotate text..........+-------------------+................8.*****.H+
| |           ..                      :                    n+1       9 ***** I|
| |          ..                Enhanced text:   x0                  10 ##### J|
| |         ..                                  Bold Italic         11 $$$$$ K|
| |        ..                                  :                    12 %%%%% L|
| |       ..                                   :                    13 @@@@@ M|
| |      .                                     :       pattern fill 14 &&&&& N|
| |     >                         + 0+ 1+ 2+ 3+ 4+ 5+ 6+ 7+ 8       15 ===== O|
| |                                 || || || || || || || || |               |
+-----linewidth lw 6----dashtype  dt 5--+-++-++-++-++-++-++-++-+-----------+
user@localhost:~/src/book$
user@localhost:~/src/book$
user@localhost:~/src/book$
```

Finally, we need an `alias` to invoke our function with the GNUTERM environment variable that's set to an acceptable graphics backend. Run the following alias with the GNUTERM variable set as determined to work with your Terminal:

```
alias gnuplot="GNUTERM=$GNUTERM __gnuplot"
```

Who, what, where, why, how?

Let's return to our book data and start to pare it down to the interesting bits. Let's look at just a little bit of our data:

```
head amazon_reviews_us_Digital_Ebook_Purchase_v1_00.tsv
```

That spat out a bunch of data with very long lines. Let's try again—maybe we really only care about the headers, so let's try this:

```
head -n1 amazon_reviews_us_Digital_Ebook_Purchase_v1_00.tsv
```

Since there's a lot of text, let's remove the text fields and focus on numeric data by removing `product_title`, `review_headline`, and `review_body`, which correspond to fields 6,13, and 14. Since we're looking at pseudo big data, let's take all the numerical or Boolean flag fields and dump all the text reviews (we can leave that for the natural-language processing folks to analyze), try this:

```
cat amazon_reviews_us_Digital_Ebook_Purchase_v1_00.tsv | cut -d $'\t' -f 4,8-12,15 > test.tsv
```

Just like that, we've reduced our data size from 6.3 GB to 383 MB of pruned `test.tsv` data, which is much more manageable. Now, let's import this into a SQL database to make aggregating tabular data as easy as a SQL query:

```
sqlite3 aws-ebook-reviews.sq3 <<EOF
.mode csv
.separator "\t"
.import test.tsv reviews
EOF
```

Let's find the products with the most reviews:

```
sqlite3 -header -column aws-ebook-reviews.sq3 " select product_id as ID, strftime('%Y-%m', review_date) DATE, star_rating as STAR, count(product_id) as COUNT from reviews group by ID order by COUNT desc limit 10"
```

The following output (counts may differ) should be displayed:

```
ID          DATE     STAR  COUNT
----------  -------- ----  ----------
B00L9B7IKE  2015-01  5     54534
B005ZOBNOI  2013-09  5     50581
B006LSZECO  2013-09  3     45467
B00BAXFECK  2013-10  5     34253
B003WUYPPG  2013-09  3     30890
B00DPM7TIG  2014-05  4     28234
B00JYWUHO4  2014-10  1     26722
B0089LOG02  2013-09  5     26155
B00CNQ7HAU  2013-10  5     24454
B004CFA9RS  2013-09  5     23677
```

54,000 reviews seems like something we could plot some interesting data for, so let's focus on the product ID B00L9B7IKE. For plotting, we know which product ID we're looking at, so let's adjust our query to not report the product ID and just focus on the dates, star rating, and counts:

```
sqlite3 -header -column aws-ebook-reviews.sq3 " select strftime('%Y-%m', review_date) DATE, star_rating as STAR, count(star_rating) as COUNT from reviews where product_id = 'B00L9B7IKE' group by DATE, STAR"
```

The following output will be displayed:

```
DATE        STAR  COUNT
----------  ----  ----------
2015-01     1     30
2015-01     2     44
2015-01     3     108
2015-01     4     304
2015-01     5     822
2015-02     1     290
2015-02     2     352
2015-02     3     818
2015-02     4     2040
2015-02     5     3466
2015-03     1     446
2015-03     2     554
2015-03     3     1294
2015-03     4     3186
2015-03     5     5092
2015-04     1     466
2015-04     2     508
2015-04     3     1178
2015-04     4     2550
2015-04     5     3806
2015-05     1     442
2015-05     2     538
2015-05     3     1152
2015-05     4     2174
2015-05     5     3058
2015-06     1     382
2015-06     2     428
2015-06     3     952
2015-06     4     1920
2015-06     5     2898
2015-07     1     388
2015-07     2     484
2015-07     3     972
2015-07     4     2122
2015-07     5     3004
```

Bash Functions and Data Visualization

```
2015-08    1 374
2015-08    2 458
2015-08    3 884
2015-08    4 1762
2015-08    5 2788
```

That's some plottable data if I've ever seen some. We can track how many reviews we're getting by day or month, and when we graph this, we can look for anomalies, such as an exceptional number of five-star reviews on a single day when prior days didn't stick out so much.

Our data still isn't quite right; for plotting, we want to group the star ratings by date in a single row, so we'll need to perform another translation on the data. We also drop the - column option so we get condensed output, and we can pipe this through `tr` when we're ready to pass the data to gnuplot. We'll also save this output into `clusterchart.dat` so that our plotting commands are short and simple:

```
sqlite3 -header aws-ebook-reviews.sq3 "select DATE, MAX(CASE WHEN STAR='1'
THEN COUNT END) as '1STAR', MAX(CASE WHEN STAR='2' THEN COUNT END) as
'2STAR', MAX(CASE WHEN STAR='3' THEN COUNT END) as '3STAR', MAX(CASE WHEN
STAR='4' THEN COUNT END) as '4STAR', MAX(CASE WHEN STAR='5' THEN COUNT END)
as '5STAR', SUM(COUNT) as TOTAL from ( select strftime('%Y-%m',
review_date) DATE, star_rating as STAR, count(star_rating) as COUNT from
reviews where product_id = 'B00L9B7IKE' group by DATE, STAR) results group
by DATE" | tr '|' '\t' > clusterchart.dat
cat clusterchart.dat
```

Finally, here's our condensed output for graphing with gnuplot:

```
DATE    1STAR 2STAR  3STAR 4STAR 5STAR   TOTAL
2015-01 30    44 108 304   822 1308
2015-02 290   352 818 2040  3466 6966
2015-03 446   554 1294 3186  5092 10572
2015-04 466   508 1178 2550  3806 8508
2015-05 442   538 1152 2174  3058 7364
2015-06 382   428 952 1920   2898 6580
2015-07 388   484 972 2122   3004 6970
2015-08 374   458 884 1762   2788 6266
```

Enter the mind's eye

Let's check out what this looks like. Run the following code:

```
gnuplot -e "set style data histograms ; set style fill solid border lt -1 ;
plot 'clusterchart.dat' using 2:xtic(1) ti col, '' u 3 ti col, '' u 4 ti
col, '' u 5 ti col, '' u 6 ti col"
```

This should produce the following in your Terminal:

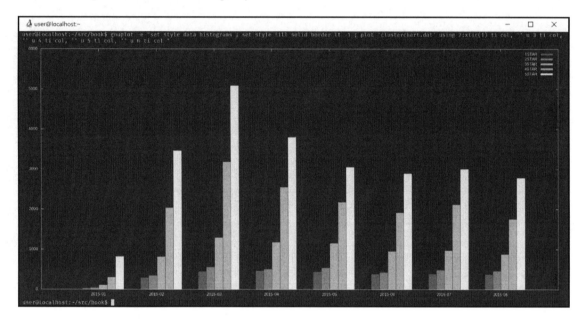

Let's do the exact same operation, but output the `dumb` output:

```
GNUTERM=dumb gnuplot -e "set style data histograms ; set style fill solid
border lt -1 ; plot 'clusterchart.dat' using 2:xtic(1) ti col, '' u 3 ti
col, '' u 4 ti col, '' u 5 ti col, '' u 6 ti col"
```

Bash Functions and Data Visualization

We get a text-based output:

To break down what we did, check out the following code:

```
GNUTERM=dumb gnuplot -e "set style data histograms ; set style fill solid
border lt -1 ; plot 'clusterchart.dat' using 2:xtic(1) ti col, '' u 3 ti
col, '' u 4 ti col, '' u 5 ti col, '' u 6 ti col"
```

The first step is to set GNUTERM, which should default to what we set in ~/.bash_profile. This tells our gnuplot wrapper which output backend to use. For GNUTERM=dumb, it will be a text backend. The next part is gnuplot with the -e expression argument. The expression is gnuplot syntax. We first set our plots to histograms instead of line graphs with set style data histograms. Next, we specify the bar color by setting it to a flood fill with a solid border and use linetype -1 as the default linetype. After we've defined our plot style, we tell gnuplot to plot our data with plot 'clusterchart.dat'. Each comma-separated parameter to plot represents a column to plot for each row of data in clusterchart.dat. We specify that the first column in our plot should use the second column of data and use the first column of data as our x-label, as denoted by 2:xtic(1) ti col.

The second column in our plot uses the same `clusterchart.dat` as input by indicating the same with two concatenated single quotes and specifies the use of the third data column for tick data. The third, fourth, and fifth columns use the same notation as the second column, which is to indicate the reuse of `clusterchart.dat` and to specify the data column to extract the y-tick data.

If we want to get a little fancier, we can use rowstacking instead of clustered bar graphs so we can visualize our data more compactly. Try this:

```
barchart -s -f clusterchart.dat 'plot for [i=2:6] $data using i:xtic(1)'
```

We get a stacked bar chart:

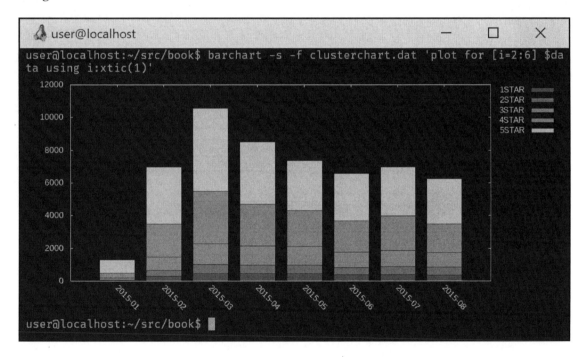

Now, if we want to see percentages, we can use our `barchart` wrapper in stacked mode. It's nice to see the discrepancy between different data segments. Try invoking the following code:

```
barchart -s -f clusterchart.dat 'plot for [i=2:6] $data using
(100.*column(i)/column(7)):xtic(1) title column(i)'
```

It produces the following output:

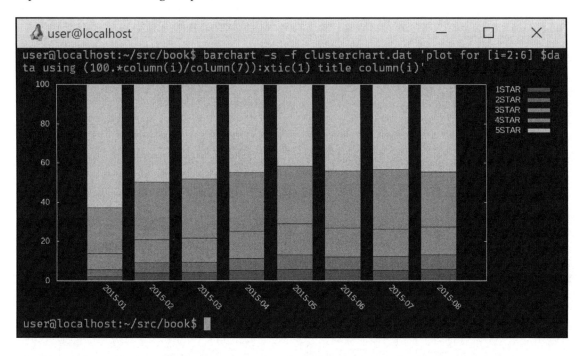

This is using our bar chart wrapper in stacked mode (-s), and specifying our `clusterchart.dat` input file, with the gnuplot script as the last parameter. For gnuplot, we're telling it to perform a single iterative plot for i=2 to 6. The `$data` variable is being set by the bar chart wrapper to the content of `clusterchart.dat`. The using parameter is multiplying our fraction by 100 to create the percentage of the bar chart for each element, i, of the total from column 7. `xtic(1)` is setting the `xtic` mark titles to the contents of column 1 for each row of data graphed in a column. In this example, we need to add the `column(i)` title to get the key title set properly to the column headers, instead of using the last referenced `column(7)` header.

Summary

With the ability to reuse bash code, a collection of scripts can be cobbled together to enhance your command-line productivity. And with the ability to visualize results, you can peer into datasets and perform data mining tasks more quickly.

In the next chapter, we'll dig deeper into bash control flow to create richer functions.

5
Loops, Functions, and String Processing

Sometimes, magic one-liners are insufficient for manipulating data. Loops and conditionals enable us to iterate over data in interesting ways without sticking to default behavior.

Bash views non-binary files and streams as collections of characters. We commonly think of these characters as groups of strings separated by some kind of whitespace. It makes sense that some of the most useful and common tools in the command-line universe are the ones that search and manipulate these strings.

The following topics will be covered in this chapter:

- `for` loops
- `while` loops
- File test conditionals
- Numeric comparisons
- String case statements
- Using regular expressions and `grep` to search and filter
- String transformations using `awk`, `sed`, and `tr`
- Sorting lists of strings with `sort` and `uniq`

Along the way, we'll see how we can pipe the results of one program into another to get the results we want.

Once, twice, three times a lady loops

Few command-line tools have implicit looping and conditionals built into them. Often, tasks will only operate on each line of an input stream and then terminate. The shell provides just enough control flow and conditionals to solve many complex problems, making up for any deficiencies that command-line tools have for operating on data.

The almighty `for` loop is a common loop idiom, however bash's `for` loop might feel a little unfamiliar to users of more traditional languages. The `for` loop allows you to iterate over a list of words, and assign each one to a variable for processing. For example, (pun intended):

```
ubuntu@commandlinebook:~$ for word in one two three; do  echo $word; done
one
two
three
ubuntu@commandlinebook:~$
```

Often, we want a more traditional range of numbers in our `for` loops. The `POSIX` method of generating a number range is to use the `seq` command, as in `seq -- $(seq 1 1 5)`, which will generate numbers from 1 (the first argument) to 5 (the third argument) in steps of 1 increment (the second argument).

In the following examples, you'll notice we are using bracket expansions, `{}`, and parentheses, `()`. For more information about both, check out `https://ss64.com/bash/syntax-brackets.html`.

Modern versions of `bash` provide an easy shorthand for this:

```
ubuntu@commandlinebook:~$ for (( i=1; i<=4; i++ )); do echo "$i"; done
1
2
3
4
ubuntu@commandlinebook:~$
```

We can also set the amount that the sequence is incremented by:

```
ubuntu@commandlinebook:~$ for i in {1..4..2}; do echo $i; done
1
3
ubuntu@commandlinebook:~$
```

Alternatively, we can use the `bash` supported C-like syntax:

```
ubuntu@commandlinebook:~$ for (( i=1; i<=4; i++ )); do echo "$i"; done
1
2
3
4
ubuntu@commandlinebook:~$
```

Looping for a specified number of times may be what we need, but we can also pass in the result of a sub-command to generate the list of things to loop over. For example, we may want to do something to each file in the current directory:

```
ubuntu@commandlinebook:~$ ls
amazon_reviews_us_Digital_Ebook_Purchase_v1_00.tsv  amazon_reviews_us_Digital_Ebook_Purchase_v1_01.tsv
ubuntu@commandlinebook:~$ for file in $(ls); do wc -l $file; done
12520723 amazon_reviews_us_Digital_Ebook_Purchase_v1_00.tsv
5101694 amazon_reviews_us_Digital_Ebook_Purchase_v1_01.tsv
ubuntu@commandlinebook:~$
```

Often, we may want to test one or more conditionals, especially in loops. Bash has an `if-then` construct, like most languages:

```
ubuntu@commandlinebook:~$ if [ -f amazon_reviews_us_Digital_Ebook_Purchase_v1_00.tsv ]; then  echo "yep"; fi
yep
ubuntu@commandlinebook:~$
```

The statement inside the brackets is a test, and bash contains a set of special tests, such as `-f` for common tasks. Here's a list of some of the most common ones:

Test type	Parameter	Description
Filesystem	-O	True if file exists and is owned by the effective user ID
Filesystem	-f	True if file exists and is a regular file
Filesystem	-G	True if file exists and is owned by the effective group ID
Filesystem	-r	True if file exists and is readable
Filesystem	-w	True if file exists and is writable
Filesystem	-x	True if file exists and is executable
Filesystem	-s	True if file exists and has a size greater than zero
Filesystem	-h	True if file exists and is a symbolic link
Arithmetic	<=	Less than equal
Arithmetic	>=	Greater than equal

Loops, Functions, and String Processing

Arithmetic	<	Less than
Arithmetic	>	Greater than
Arithmetic	!=	Not equal
Arithmetic	=	Equal

Like other languages, we can also include `else-if` tests, and finally an `else if` nothing else matches:

```
ubuntu@commandlinebook:~$ if [ 0 = 1 ]; then echo "a"; elif [ 0 = 2 ]; then echo "b"; else echo "c"; fi
c
ubuntu@commandlinebook:~$
```

Even though the `if-else` construct exists, most shell scripts use the pipeline semantics of `&&` (AND) and `||` (OR). We briefly mentioned this in Chapter 3, *Obtaining and Working with Data and Detached Processing and Terminal Multiplexers*, but here's a more detailed example:

```
[ 0 = 1 ] && echo "a" || ([0==2] && echo b || echo c)
[ -f /myconfig ] && read_params /myconfig
```

It's the end of the world as we know it while and until

Let's explore two more options for assisting with iteration. The `while` construct allows for the repetitive execution of a list or set of commands as long as the command that controls the `while` loop exits successfully. Let's see an example:

Let's say I wanted to print the `"hello!"` string four times in a script—no more and no less. We can do so with the following:

```
1 while.sh +
#!/bin/bash

i="0"

while [ $i -lt 4 ]
do
echo "Hello!" &
i=$[$i+1]
done
```

Let's save and run this script to see what happens.

 Don't forget to `chmod -x` these scripts to make them executable.

Executing the script produces the following:

```
ubuntu@commandlinebook:~$ ./while.sh
hello!
hello!
hello!
hello!
ubuntu@commandlinebook:~$
```

Notice that, in the script, we created a variable called `i="0"`. This sets the `i` variable to zero. Do you see the `while [ $i -lt 4 ]` block? This allows us to run the loop as the `i` variable is less than the `4` integer. Go ahead and play around with this code for a bit to get a better understanding. Also, you can `man [` for more information.

Loops, Functions, and String Processing

In our while script, we counted up until four for our output. Let's use the `until` construct to count down and provide the `goodbye!` output:

```
1 until.sh
#!/bin/bash

i="20"

until [ $i -lt 10 ]
do
echo "Goodbye!" &
let i-=1
done
```

Let's save and run this script to see what happens:

```
ubuntu@commandlinebook:~$ ./until.sh
goodbye!
goodbye!
goodbye!
goodbye!
goodbye!
goodbye!
goodbye!
goodbye!
goodbye!
goodbye!
ubuntu@commandlinebook:~$ goodbye!
```

The simple case

Frequently, string comparison is done using the test operator, `[`. This is ill-advised in bash, as there's a much more convenient format for string comparison, using the `case` statement. Here's a simple example:

```
testcase() {
for VAR; do
case "${VAR}" in
        '') echo "empty";;
        a) echo "a";;
```

```
            b) echo "b";;
            c) echo "c";;
            *) echo "not a, b, c";;
    esac
    done
    }
    testcase '' foo a bar b c d
```

The `testcase` function lets us test the `case` statement by wrapping it in a `for` loop that assigns each function argument to the `VAR` variable, then executes the `case` statement. With the `foo a bar b c d` arguments, we can expect the following output:

```
empty
not a, b, c
a
not a, b, c
b
c
d
```

Pay no heed to the magician redirecting your attention

Looping is great for working over sequences of data in an iterative fashion, but sometimes, when you're doing all that work, you get lots of irrelevant output. Enter our little magician: the output redirection operator, >. This operator directs output to a specified file or file descriptor. We've talked about file descriptors, they are integers that the OS uses to identify a file handle that has been opened, and by default there are three opened for every process: `stdin`, `stdout`, and `stderr`. The default file descriptors, denoted by `fd#`, are `fd0` for standard input, `fd1` for standard output, and `fd2` for standard error. The > operator by default, redirects `stdout`, the equivalent of `1>`, unless it's preceded by an integer file-descriptor. Let's see some examples of output redirection, before we get lost in what we're referring to:

```
ls /
ls / >/dev/null
ls /foobar 2>/dev/null
ls / /foobar >stdout_and_stderr.log 2>&1
ls / /foobar >stdout.log 2>stderr.log
ls / /foobar 2>&1 >/dev/null
```

Loops, Functions, and String Processing

Normal messaging is sent to standard output, and is rendered as text in your Terminal window. This is how `ls /` will show the contents of the root filesystem to your Terminal. In the second invocation, we use `>` to indicate that `stdout` should be redirected to `/dev/null`, which will discard the output. The third sends error messages to `dev/null`, so they don't render to the Terminal. The fourth example redirects `stdout` to a file named `stdout_and_stderr.log` and then copies `stderr` to the same location as `stdout` with `&1`. The fifth example splits `stdout` to `stdout.log` and `stderr` to `stderr.log`. The sixth example doesn't redirect `stderr` to `/dev/null`, rather it redirects `stderr` to where `stdout` is pointing at the time of the assignment—the Terminal and then `stdout` is redirected to `/dev/null`. This shows that the order of operators matters and diligence should be paid to ensure that assignments occur in definition order. The last point to make is that because `stdout` is a file descriptor, and not the Terminal, it's possible to direct other output to the Terminal, and have `stdout` directed to another file descriptor that won't result in Terminal output.

There are three less-frequently-used redirection operators: `<` for input redirection, `>>` for output append redirection, and `<<` for HEREDOC. Input redirection is used to feed data into a pipeline, like this:

```
cat <stdout.log | grep lines
```

This will read `stdout.log` into the standard input of the `cat` command, which will write its output to the pipe operator. There's really not much more to input redirection, as pipelines implicitly set the `stdout` of the previous command to the standard input of the next command. We also mentioned the append operator, `>>`, and it's necessary to point out that the `>` redirection operator truncates files to zero content before writing. This behavior isn't desired if data needs to be preserved between runs. To clarify, this truncates data in `keys.log`:

```
grep keyword > keys.log
```

The other option is appending the following:

```
grep keyword >> keys.log
```

Lastly, the `heredoc` operator, `<<`, it replaces standard input with a predefined text-stream book ended by a keyword that follows `<< KEYWORD`. For example, the following example can be used to truncate an `options.conf` file and write the three option values into the file:

```
cat <<EOF >options.conf
option=true
option2=false
option3=cat
EOF
```

Regular expressions and grep

One key task you will face over and over is matching particular patterns of text. The match might be as simple as finding one instance of a specific string in a body of text, or it could be much more complicated. A great tool for matching text is the language of regular expressions. A regular expression is an abstract way of expressing certain types of string-matching patterns.

Contrary to popular belief, regular expressions can't match everything you might want to match. They're limited to certain types of matches, and depending on the particular flavor of regular expression implementation, they could have a little more or a little less power. As an academic exercise, one might try to characterize exactly what you can match and what you can't. It's a very interesting endeavor that cuts to the very core of theoretical computer science. But we won't be doing that here: we are here to do practical things!

First up, you'll want to find a way to test your regular expressions. There are several tools available on the web that allow you to interactively test your matches. A couple of good ones are listed at the end of this section. Of course, this is a command-line book, and you can test matches yourself just by putting test text in a file and using `grep`. Grep is a program that takes a regular expression and emits the lines in the input stream that match that regular expression (by default, it emits lines where any substring of the line matches the regular expression).

Exact matches

A regular expression is a string itself. Several characters are reserved, that is, when they're present in the string, they have a special meaning. Any non-reserved character in the `regex` must be matched exactly, in the exact order that it appears. Notably, a `regex` that's nothing but a normal character must be an exact match on the entire string.

You do multiple things with a `regex`. Sometimes, you may require that the entire target strings match. Other times, you may want to find if and where a substring of the target string matches.

Here's a table of `regex` pattern matches:

Regex	String	Matches?	Matches substring?
abc	abc	Yes	Yes
abc	abcd	No	Yes (abcd)
abc	def	No	No

Let's look for an exact match on the `aardvark` string in the review titles of our test dataset:

```
zcat amazon_reviews_us_Digital_Ebook_Purchase_v1_01.tsv.gz | cut -f13 | grep aardvark
```

The red-highlighted content is the matched content:

```
ubuntu@commandlinebook:~$ zcat amazon_reviews_us_Digital_Ebook_Purchase_v1_01.tsv.gz | cut -f13 | grep aardvark
aardvarkingly absolutely great
May an aardvark follow the author, and keep all his pic-nics free of ants.
ubuntu@commandlinebook:~$
```

Character sets

After an exact string, you might want to match one of a couple of characters instead of one exactly. To do this, we use the `characters []` bracket to enclose the list of characters that we might want to match. We can only match one of the possible characters inside the brackets.

Here's a table of `regex` pattern matches:

Regex	String	Matches?	Matches substring?
ab[cd]	abc	Yes	Yes
ab[cd]	abcd	No	Yes (abcd)
ab[cd]	abe	No	No

Let's see whether there are any examples of a capitalized `aardvark` in our review data:

```
zcat amazon_reviews_us_Digital_Ebook_Purchase_v1_01.tsv.gz | cut -f13 |
grep [Aa]ardvark
```

The red-highlighted content is the matched content:

```
ubuntu@commandlinebook:~$ zcat amazon_reviews_us_Digital_Ebook_Purchase_v1_01.tsv.gz | cut -f13 | grep [Aa]ardvark
review - Yes, We Treat Aardvarks
Yea, We Treat Aardvarks by Robert M. Miller DVM
aardvarkingly absolutely great
May an aardvark follow the author, and keep all his pic-nics free of ants.
ubuntu@commandlinebook:~$
```

Dot the i (or anything else)

The dot character, `.`, is a one-character wildcard character. It will match anything. There are also restricted wildcards that only match certain types of characters: `\d` matches a digit, `\w` matches any alphanumeric character or an underscore, and `\s` matches whitespace.

Here's a table of `regex` pattern matches:

Regex	String	Matches?	Matches substring?
\s..ick	The trick	Yes	Yes
...	abcd	No	Yes (abcd)
abc\ddef	abc_def	No	No

We could have done the last search for a capital A (or anything else starting our `ardvark` string) using a dot:

```
zcat amazon_reviews_us_Digital_Ebook_Purchase_v1_01.tsv.gz | cut -f13 |
grep .ardvark
```

The red-highlighted content is the matched content:

```
ubuntu@commandlinebook:~$ zcat amazon_reviews_us_Digital_Ebook_Purchase_v1_01.tsv.gz | cut -f13 | grep .ardvark
review - Yes, We Treat Aardvarks
Yea, We Treat Aardvarks by Robert M. Miller DVM
aardvarkingly absolutely great
May an aardvark follow the author, and keep all his pic-nics free of ants.
ubuntu@commandlinebook:~$
```

Capture groups

We can set apart groups of characters with parentheses. While not terribly useful on their own, these groups can be combined with other operators to do very useful things. We call these groups capture groups because the `regex` engine captures what was matched inside the group. Later on, you can use what was captured to match something else.

We will show some examples of using capture groups later, in the section on `awk`.

Either or, neither nor

The pipe character, `|`, lets us match one or the other of something. We can delineate where the pair starts by using a capture group. Invoke the following:

```
zcat amazon_reviews_us_Digital_Ebook_Purchase_v1_01.tsv.gz | cut -f13 |
grep -E '(aardvark|giraffe)'
```

The red-highlighted content is the matched content:

```
ubuntu@commandlinebook:~$ zcat amazon_reviews_us_Digital_Ebook_Purchase_v1_01.tsv.gz | cut -f13 | grep -E '(aardvark|giraffe)'
The white giraffe
Cute giraffe photos that kids love
Tears of the giraffe
felly the tiny giraffe
Shortgiraffe
Good giraffe
aardvarkingly absolutely great
May an aardvark follow the author, and keep all his pic-nics free of ants.
white giraffe is great
I loved the giraffe
A big "giraffe"??
the white giraffe
the white giraffe
ubuntu@commandlinebook:~$
```

[78]

Repetition

There are three heavily-used operators that let us match repetitions. They are the question mark, ?, the plus, +, and the asterisk, *.

The question mark, ?, matches exactly 0 or 1 instances of the thing it's applied to (a character, set, or group). Invoke the following:

```
zcat amazon_reviews_us_Digital_Ebook_Purchase_v1_01.tsv.gz | cut -f13 |
grep -E '(a)?ardvark'
```

The red-highlighted content is the matched content:

```
ubuntu@commandlinebook:~$ zcat amazon_reviews_us_Digital_Ebook_Purchase_v1_01.tsv.gz | cut -f13 | grep -E '(a)?ardvark'
review - Yes, We Treat Aardvarks
Yea, We Treat Aardvarks by Robert M. Miller DVM
aardvarkingly absolutely great
May an aardvark follow the author, and keep all his pic-nics free of ants.
ubuntu@commandlinebook:~$
```

The plus operator, +, matches one or more things, and the asterisk operator, *, matches 0 or more things. Invoke the following:

```
zcat amazon_reviews_us_Digital_Ebook_Purchase_v1_01.tsv.gz | cut -f13 |
grep -E 'aaaaaaa(a)*' | head -n 3
```

It produces this output:

```
ubuntu@commandlinebook:~$ zcat amazon_reviews_us_Digital_Ebook_Purchase_v1_01.tsv.gz | cut -f13 | grep -E 'aaaaaaa(a)*' | head -n 3
Aaaaaaaaaahhhhhhh, much better!
Whaaaaaaatttt?!?!?!?!
Maaaaaaaan
ubuntu@commandlinebook:~$
```

Other operators

You can match many things with regex, and each implementation of regex is a little different. I suggest looking at these resources for a full treatment of each kind of regex and what you can do with them:

- A great, comprehensive site with many examples: https://www.regular-expressions.info/
- A site to test and debug different types of regex: https://regex101.com/
- Another regex test site: https://www.regexpal.com/
- A library of regex instances that others have created: http://www.regexlib.com

[79]

Loops, Functions, and String Processing

Putting it all together

As a recap, we have the following operators:

Operator	Use
`Brackets []`	Specifies sets of characters to match
`Capture Group ()`	Groups characters, and pulls out what was matched later
`Or |`	Matches one of two things
`?`	Matches zero or one times
`+`	Matches one or more times
`*`	Matches zero or more times

awk, sed, and tr

In this section, we will be looking at `awk`, `sed`, and `tr`.

awk

`awk` (including the `gnu` implementation, `gawk`) is designed for streaming text processing, data extraction, and reporting. An `awk` program is structured as a set of patterns that are matched, and actions to take when those patterns are matched:

```
pattern {action}
pattern {action}
pattern {action}
...
```

For each record (usually each line of text passed to `awk`), each pattern is tested to see whether the record matches, and if so, the action is taken. Additionally, each record is automatically split into a list of fields by a delimiter (any run of whitespace by default). The default action, if none is given, is to print the record. The default pattern is to match everything. There are two special patterns, `BEGIN` and `END`, which are matched only before any records are processed, or after, respectively.

`awk` is very good at doing certain kinds of math on input streams, which we'll discuss later in the book. For strings, `awk` is great at filtering an input stream on complex conditions, doing transformations on input data, and combinations of these things.

Filtering on a complex condition is as easy as supplying the filter condition as a pattern and the default action (which is to say, nothing). `awk` will then, by default, print out the whole line. As an example, we might want to simulate grep by matching on a regular expression:

```
zcat amazon_reviews_us_Digital_Ebook_Purchase_v1_01.tsv.gz | cut -f13 | awk '/aardvark/'
```

The preceding code produces this:

```
ubuntu@commandlinebook:~$ zcat amazon_reviews_us_Digital_Ebook_Purchase_v1_01.tsv.gz | cut -f13 | awk '/aardvark/'
aardvarkingly absolutely great
May an aardvark follow the author, and keep all his pic-nics free of ants.
ubuntu@commandlinebook:~$
```

Here, the forward slashes indicate that the string inside is a `regex`. We can even get rid of `cut` here, as `awk` itself can look for the tab field separators. If we do this, we need to tell `awk` that we're looking for substrings of the appropriate field. The special variables, `$1`, `$2`, and so on, represent the fields of each record. `$0` is the entire record. Invoke the following:

```
zcat amazon_reviews_us_Digital_Ebook_Purchase_v1_01.tsv.gz | awk -F"\t" '$13 ~ /aardvark/'
```

The preceding code produces this:

```
ubuntu@commandlinebook:~$ zcat amazon_reviews_us_Digital_Ebook_Purchase_v1_01.tsv.gz | awk -F"\t" '$13 ~ /aardvark/'
US    41926810   R3BTQZHST3RVCL  B002B0LYHI  144519531  Sea of Monsters, The (Percy Jackson and the Olympians, Book 2)  Digital_Ebook_Purchase  5  0  0
N   N   aardvarkingly absolutely great  sometimes when i read this book i cry. my dream? to save the WORLD. to have great powers. i want it to be real so badly . and i w
ish it was real but i read all the books and i know the future. but i would watch. and i would help percy! basically im sure that im the biggest fan because ive reread the ligh
tning thief exactly 137 times. im SO not kidding. ive kept track and i AM an extremley fast reader  must read the book. i KNOW you think its dorky geeky and nerdy. umm....NO IT
ISNT.  2012-11-07
US    26712568   R2KBY7HIE29DF8  B008KLT9M6  670479126  Curses and Blessings for All Occasions  Digital_Ebook_Purchase  5   2   2   N   N
ay an aardvark follow the author, and keep all his pic-nics free of ants.   I was blessed to get this free in a kindle edition . It is superb! There is an originality that
it rarely found these days, and the humour is brilliant!<br />i follow st on gocomics.  and would never miss a panel. Plus, for purists, the artwork is outstanding.  2012-08-
20
ubuntu@commandlinebook:~$
```

We printed the entire record here since we didn't cut it in advance, and we told `awk` to do the default, which is printing the entire record. Maybe we want to just print out the title, field 6, when we match `aardvark` in the review description. We have to add a non-default action to our filter:

```
> zcat amazon_reviews_us_Digital_Ebook_Purchase_v1_01.tsv.gz | awk -F"\t" '$13 ~ /aardvark/ {print $6}'
```

The preceding code generates this output:

```
ubuntu@commandlinebook:~$ zcat amazon_reviews_us_Digital_Ebook_Purchase_v1_01.tsv.gz | awk -F"\t" '$13 ~ /aardvark/ {print $6}'
Sea of Monsters, The (Percy Jackson and the Olympians, Book 2)
Curses and Blessings for All Occasions
ubuntu@commandlinebook:~$
```

Loops, Functions, and String Processing

We can also do things such as picking out the fields we want, re-ordering them, and printing them out with a different field separator which we define in the BEGIN pattern:

```
> zcat amazon_reviews_us_Digital_Ebook_Purchase_v1_01.tsv.gz | awk -F"\t"
'BEGIN {OFS=";"} ; $13 ~ /aardvark/ {print $6, $2, $3}'
```

The preceding code looks like this in the Terminal:

> More information on awk can be found at https://www.gnu.org/software/gawk/manual/gawk.html.

sed

sed is an alternative to awk for line-by-line stream editing. One of the most common uses of sed is for easy regex replacement. For example, we can pipe the strings that contain aardvark that we found in the review descriptions and replace them with giraffe:

```
zcat amazon_reviews_us_Digital_Ebook_Purchase_v1_01.tsv.gz | cut -f13 | awk
'/aardvark/' | sed 's/aardvark/giraffe/g'
```

The preceding code should output the following:

sed can also delete lines matching a pattern:

```
zcat amazon_reviews_us_Digital_Ebook_Purchase_v1_01.tsv.gz | cut -f13 | awk
'/aardvark/' | sed '/ant/d'
```

The preceding code produces this output:

Sed has almost 30 commands in addition to more complex stream processing.

 More information on sed can be found at https://www.gnu.org/software/sed/manual/sed.html.

tr

The `tr` command is somewhat simpler than `awk` or `sed`, but sometimes it's just what's needed: `tr` translates or deletes characters from a stream.

Say we really hate the letter `a` and we'd like to replace all of them with `b`. With `tr`, this is simple:

```
zcat amazon_reviews_us_Digital_Ebook_Purchase_v1_01.tsv.gz | cut -f13 | awk '/aardvark/' | tr 'a' 'b'
```

The preceding code produces this output:

```
ubuntu@commandlinebook:~$ zcat amazon_reviews_us_Digital_Ebook_Purchase_v1_01.tsv.gz | cut -f13 | awk '/aardvark/' | tr 'a' 'b'
bbrdvbrkingly bbsolutely grebt
Mby bn bbrdvbrk follow the buthor, bnd keep bll his pic-nics free of bnts.
ubuntu@commandlinebook:~$
```

sort and uniq

After `awk`, `sed`, and `tr`, `sort`, and `uniq` are going to be a breeze.

sort

`sort`, well, sorts a stream of strings (or numbers). It won't remove duplicates, it keeps them. By default, `sort` puts things in alphabetical order.

We can see `sort` in action by piping one column of data (using `cut`) from a few lines (using `head`) from our example data:

```
zcat amazon_reviews_us_Digital_Ebook_Purchase_v1_01.tsv.gz | head -n 10 | cut -f13 | sort
```

The preceding code produces this output:

```
ubuntu@commandlinebook:~$ zcat amazon_reviews_us_Digital_Ebook_Purchase_v1_01.tsv.gz | head -n 10 | cut -f13 | sort
Awesome book
Barbarians
Face of betrayal
Menu....
Quirky
review_headline
Steamy and suspenseful!!!!!
The Woman Who Wasn't There
This Sleepy Sheep rocks!
Very good
ubuntu@commandlinebook:~$
```

If you pass `sort` the `-n` flag, it will `sort` numerically instead:

```
zcat amazon_reviews_us_Digital_Ebook_Purchase_v1_01.tsv.gz | head -n 10 |
tail -n +2 | cut -f13,8 | sort -n
```

The preceding code produces this output:

```
ubuntu@commandlinebook:~$ zcat amazon_reviews_us_Digital_Ebook_Purchase_v1_01.tsv.gz | head -n 10 | tail -n +2 | cut -f13,8 | sort -n
3       Menu....
4       Quirky
4       The Woman Who Wasn't There
5       Awesome book
5       Barbarians
5       Face of betrayal
5       Steamy and suspenseful!!!!!
5       This Sleepy Sheep rocks!
5       Very good
ubuntu@commandlinebook:~$
```

Sometimes, you might want to sort on just a part of the data. In this way, you can start to treat these streams of data more like a database. You can use the `-k` option to sort data by columns, along with the `-t` option if your data is delimited by something other than tabs. We can use this, for example, to find the review with the most helpful votes:

```
zcat amazon_reviews_us_Digital_Ebook_Purchase_v1_01.tsv.gz | head -n 50000
| tail -n +2 | sort -t$'\t' -k9n,9   | tail -n 1
```

The preceding code produces lots of output:

```
ubuntu@commandlinebook:~$ zcat amazon_reviews_us_Digital_Ebook_Purchase_v1_01.tsv.gz | head -n 50000 | tail -n +2 | sort -t$'\t' -k9n,9 | tail -n 1
US      52955558        R154S53MBJEJMP  B008UUIG87      80194507        I Bring the Fire Part I  Wolves (A Loki Series)    Digital_Ebook_Purchase   3      250     279
       Not a complete story on its own I was really enjoying this story.  And then it stopped.  Not even a mini-conclusion to any plot line, just buy the next book if you want
 to see what happens.  It felt as though there was a scissors after some random number of pages and that was the end of this book.<br /><br />I think that's a cheat, and there
 is no reason to think there will be an actual conclusion to the next one either, so even though I really like the promise and these characters, I am out.   2013-09-08
ubuntu@commandlinebook:~$
```

Here, we pass the `-k9n,9` option to sort from column 9 to column 9 (just the one column), and we pass `n` to sort numerically.

You can also sort on more than one column. Say we wanted to sort first by column 9 descending, but them by column 10 ascending:

```
zcat amazon_reviews_us_Digital_Ebook_Purchase_v1_01.tsv.gz | head -n 50000
| tail -n +2 | sort -t$'\t' -k9nr,9 -k10n,10  | tail -n 1
```

The preceding code produces the following output:

In this example, we found the review with the least helpful votes but the most total votes as a tiebreak.

uniq

`uniq` is a funny little program that usually just removes adjacent identical lines in a stream of data. We put it in with `sort` because, usually, you see it used with data piped from `sort` to count the unique values in a stream of data:

```
zcat amazon_reviews_us_Digital_Ebook_Purchase_v1_01.tsv.gz | head -n 50000
| tail -n +2 | cut -f8 | sort | uniq
```

It produces this counting sequence:

We can see the only possible star ratings are 1 through 5.

`uniq` has some other uses, but this is by far the main use of `uniq`.

Summary

In this chapter, we covered the breadth of bash's control structures and dived into input/output redirection. These features can be leveraged to enhance your command-line functions and enable small scripts that process data in loops without having to resort to a full-fledged programming language for some simple data processing.

We also looked at a lot of ways to slice and dice characters and strings. While many use cases may be covered using string manipulation alone, often we'll want to delve a little deeper into the data represented by these streams to extract useful information.

In the next chapter, we'll look at doing this by using the command line and data streams as a database.

6
SQL, Math, and Wrapping it up

Databases are attractive solutions for storing and accessing data. They supply the developer with an API that allows the structured organization of data, the ability to search that data in flexible ways, and the ability to store new data. When a database's capabilities are a requirement, there's often little room left for negotiation; the question is which database and not whether we should use one.

Despite this fact, the Unix command line provides a suite of tools that lets a developer view streams or files in many of the same ways as they would view a database. Given one or more files with data in it, we can use these tools to query that data without ever having to maintain a database or any of the things that go along with it, such as fixed schemas. Often, we can use this method for processing data instead of standing up a database server and dealing with the issues associated with the **Extract**, **Transformation**, and **Load** (**ETL**) of data into that database. Even better, our pipeline, and therefore our view of the data, can change over time, unlike the relatively static schemas of traditional databases.

Often, you'll need to perform computations on numerical data in your workflows. The command line has several tools that enable us to do this.

Bash itself has the capability to do some math in shell scripts. When a little more capability is required, two command-line tools, `bc` and `awk`, are capable of doing many types of calculations.

Sometimes, we may need the full power of a programming language and mathematics packages, such as Python and Pandas. While this isn't a tutorial on how to do data science in Python, in this chapter, we'll see how to interface your Python routines in line with other command-line tools and build a custom pipeline for your needs.

SQL, Math, and Wrapping it up

We'll also be using many of the tools that we have seen in this book to perform some real-world analysis on weather data.

So, to sum it up, in this chapter we will be looking at:

- Viewing data as columns using `cut`
- Using `grep` as a `WHERE` clause
- Joining different sets of data using the `join` command
- Simulating `SELECT` clauses using `awk`
- Learning how to use SQLite when a more fully-featured database is needed
- Bash variable assignment
- Basic bash arithmetic and comparisons
- Math using `bc`
- Streaming calculations with `awk`
- Interfacing with python routines
- Looking at the contents of a publicly available weather API
- Scraping the API and storing the results in lightweight databases
- Using the tools discussed in the previous chapters to analyze the data in the databases we've created
- Drawing some conclusions about how accurate the weather forecast is

cut and viewing data as columnar

The first thing you will likely need to do is partition data in files into rows of data and columns of data. We saw some transformations in the previous chapters that allow us to manipulate data one row at a time. For this chapter, we'll assume the rows of your data correspond with the lines of data in your files. If this isn't the case, this may be the first thing you want to do in your pipeline.

Given that we have some rows of data in our file or stream, we would like to view those rows in a columnar fashion, such as a traditional database. We can do this using the help of the `cut` command. `cut` will allow us to chop the lines of the file into columns by a delimiter, and to select which of those columns get passed through to the output.

If your data is a comma-separated or tab-separated file, `cut` is quite simple:

```
zcat amazon_reviews_us_Digital_Ebook_Purchase_v1_01.tsv.gz | cut -d$'\t' -f2,8 | head
```

The preceding code produces these results:

```
ubuntu@commandlinebook:~$ zcat amazon_reviews_us_Digital_Ebook_Purchase_v1_01.tsv.gz | cut -d$'\t' -f2,8 | head
customer_id     star_rating
33605939        4
34058393        4
39601147        5
17351407        5
10463387        5
50484904        3
7145636 5
6285538 5
10278048        5
ubuntu@commandlinebook:~$
```

In this command, we're telling `cut` that the delimiter is using `-d$'\t'`. Also, we use the `-f2,8` option to tell `cut` which of the columns we would like to pass from the input to the output. Note that we captured the header row of the data, which probably isn't desired. To skip it, add `tail -n +2` to the pipe:

```
zcat amazon_reviews_us_Digital_Ebook_Purchase_v1_01.tsv.gz | cut -d$'\t' -f2,8 | tail -n +2 | head
```

The preceding code produces these results:

```
ubuntu@commandlinebook:~$ zcat amazon_reviews_us_Digital_Ebook_Purchase_v1_01.tsv.gz | cut -d$'\t' -f2,8 | tail -n +2 | head
33605939        4
34058393        4
39601147        5
17351407        5
10463387        5
50484904        3
7145636 5
6285538 5
10278048        5
16568972        4
ubuntu@commandlinebook:~$
```

If your line is more complicated than a CSV or TSV, you may have to do more than one pass using cut, or possibly an intervening step using `awk` or `sed`. For example, in the book-review dataset, say we want to output the date field, but in year-month-date order. We can first select down to the date field, re-cut the date field into its constituent parts, and output them in the desired order:

```
zcat amazon_reviews_us_Digital_Ebook_Purchase_v1_01.tsv.gz | cut -d$'\t' -f15 | cut -d$'-' -f2,3,1 | head
```

SQL, Math, and Wrapping it up

The preceding code produces these results:

```
ubuntu@commandlinebook:~$ zcat amazon_reviews_us_Digital_Ebook_Purchase_v1_01.tsv.gz | cut -d$'\t' -f15 | cut -d$'-' -f2,3,1 | head
review_date
2013-09-09
2013-09-09
2013-09-09
2013-09-09
2013-09-09
2013-09-09
2013-09-09
2013-09-09
2013-09-09
ubuntu@commandlinebook:~$
```

`cut` can also cut particular bytes or characters from a stream if you have fixed-width fields:

```
zcat amazon_reviews_us_Digital_Ebook_Purchase_v1_01.tsv.gz | cut -c1-12 | head
```

The preceding code produces these results:

```
ubuntu@commandlinebook:~$ zcat amazon_reviews_us_Digital_Ebook_Purchase_v1_01.tsv.gz | cut -c1-12 | head
marketplace
US      33605939
US      34058393
US      39601147
US      17351407
US      10463387
US      50484904
US      7145636 R
US      6285538 R
US      10278048
ubuntu@commandlinebook:~$
```

In the case of the book data, this isn't going to make much sense since the fields are variable-width, but sometimes it's just what you need.

Using `cut` in this fashion will be your tool for a SQL-like `SELECT` of particular characters in each row of your data.

WHERE clauses

The powerful grep regular-expression-matching tool we discussed in a previous chapter allows us to perform `WHERE` clauses on our files. The clause may be a bit less intuitive than a SQL `WHERE` clause, but we can do as much or more with grep as we can with the SQL `WHERE` clause. For example, perhaps we only care about accounts starting with the number 3:

```
zcat amazon_reviews_us_Digital_Ebook_Purchase_v1_01.tsv.gz | cut -d$'\t' -f2,8 | tail -n +2 | grep "^3" | head
```

The following will be displayed on your screen:

```
ubuntu@commandlinebook:~$ zcat amazon_reviews_us_Digital_Ebook_Purchase_v1_01.tsv.gz | cut -d$'\t' -f2,8 | tail -n +2 | grep "^3" | head
33605939        4
34058393        4
39601147        5
34645512        5
37288345        5
39885508        5
34092809        5
37746905        5
30306974        4
39575324        1
ubuntu@commandlinebook:~$
```

Join, for joining data

Join works how an INNER JOIN might work in your SQL-style database. Two sorted files or streams are passed to the join command (see the section on sort to see how to sort your streams). The lines of the files must be sorted on the field you are attempting to join on. The join command will then output the results of the inner join on these two files, where if there's a matching field it will output the join key along with the remainder of the data lines of the first file concatenated with the second.

For example, say we would like to find users who are present both in the first review file and the second, and how many reviews they have in each. We can run the following join command:

```
join -j2 <(zcat amazon_reviews_us_Digital_Ebook_Purchase_v1_01.tsv.gz | cut -d$'\t' -f2 | sort | uniq -c) <(zcat amazon_reviews_us_Digital_Ebook_Purchase_v1_00.tsv.gz | cut -d$'\t' -f2 | sort | uniq -c) | head
```

The preceding code produces these results:

```
ubuntu@commandlinebook:~$ join -j2 <(zcat amazon_reviews_us_Digital_Ebook_Purchase_v1_01.tsv.gz | cut -d$'\t' -f2 | sort | uniq -c) <(zcat amazon_reviews_us_Digital_Ebook_Pur
ase_v1_00.tsv.gz | cut -d$'\t' -f2 | sort | uniq -c) | head
10000105 1 2
10000144 1 128
10000155 2 1
10000185 5 2
10000208 1 6
10000220 1 1
10000221 2 1
10000326 4 5
10000328 1 1
10000376 1 3
ubuntu@commandlinebook:~$
```

Here, we're using process substitution to slice the review files' data. This is done in parallel, increasing the speed of the process.

Group by and ordering

We can perform a GROUP BY operation by using sort piped to uniq -c (as discussed in Chapter 5, *Loops, Functions, and String Processing*):

```
zcat amazon_reviews_us_Digital_Ebook_Purchase_v1_01.tsv.gz | cut -d$'\t' -f
2 | sort | uniq -c | head
```

The preceding code produces these results:

```
ubuntu@commandlinebook:~$ zcat amazon_reviews_us_Digital_Ebook_Purchase_v1_01.tsv.gz | cut -d$'\t' -f 2 | sort | uniq -c | head
      2 10000026
      1 10000064
      1 10000073
      1 10000105
      1 10000113
      1 10000144
      2 10000155
      2 10000157
      1 10000163
      1 10000168
ubuntu@commandlinebook:~$
```

In the preceding example, we are simply counting how many reviews each user made. We might want to get the average review of each user, which can be done using awk associative arrays:

```
zcat amazon_reviews_us_Digital_Ebook_Purchase_v1_01.tsv.gz | cut -d$'\t' -
f2,8 | awk '{sum[$1]+=$2;count[$1]+=1} END {for (i in sum) {print
i,sum[i],count[i],sum[i]/count[i]}}' | head
```

The preceding code produces these results:

```
ubuntu@commandlinebook:~$ zcat amazon_reviews_us_Digital_Ebook_Purchase_v1_01.tsv.gz | cut -d$'\t' -f2,8 | awk '{sum[$1]+=$2;count[$1]+=1} END {for (i in sum) {print i,sum[i],
count[i],sum[i]/count[i]}}' | head
50185427 8 3 2.66667
38368034 4 1 4
35462117 24 5 4.8
11929143 10 2 5
46275783 15 3 5
11929144 15 3 5
44648357 5 1 5
19085804 5 1 5
12065128 1 1 1
19185935 13 3 4.33333
ubuntu@commandlinebook:~$
```

Here, the output of the command is the ID, the sum of the reviews, the count of the reviews, and the average review for each user.

We can also sort the resulting data using the same tool, sort. For example, we can take our preceding GROUP BY example, and ORDER BY the number of reviews each user made to find the most prolific reviewers:

```
zcat amazon_reviews_us_Digital_Ebook_Purchase_v1_01.tsv.gz | cut -d$'\t' -
f2,8 | awk '{sum[$1]+=$2;count[$1]+=1} END {for (i in sum) {print
i,sum[i],count[i],sum[i]/count[i]}}' | sort -k3 -r -n | head
```

The preceding code produces these results:

The number of reviews each user made to find the most prolific reviewers

Simulating selects

In the previous sections, we saw how to SELECT data, inner JOIN data, and even do GROUP BY and ORDER BY operations on flat files or streams of data. Rounding out the commonly-used operations, we can also create sub-selected tables of data by simply wrapping a set of calls into a stream and then processing them further. This is what we've been doing using the piping model, but to illustrate a point, say we wanted to sub-select out of the grouped-by reviews only those reviewers who had between 100 and 200 reviews. We can take the command in the preceding example and awk it once more:

```
zcat amazon_reviews_us_Digital_Ebook_Purchase_v1_01.tsv.gz | cut -d$'\t' -
f2,8 | awk '{sum[$1]+=$2;count[$1]+=1} END {for (i in sum) {print
i,sum[i],count[i],sum[i]/count[i]}}' | sort -k3 -r -n | awk '$3 >= 100 &&
$3 <=200' | head
```

The preceding code produces these results:

Sub-selecting out of the grouped-by reviews only those reviewers who had between 100 and 200 reviews

Using all of these tools, you saw how we can simulate most of the common SQL expressions on rows of file or stream data using the command line.

Keys to the kingdom

Now that we can explore data with the command line and have mastered transforming text, we'll provide you with the keys to the kingdom. SQLite is a public domain library that implements a SQL engine and provides a `sqlite` command shell for interacting with database files. Unlike Oracle, MySQL, and other database engines that provide a network endpoint, sqlite is offline and locally driven by library calls to interact with a single file that is the entire database. This makes backups easy. Backups can be created by doing `cp database.sq3 backups/`date +%F`-database.sq3`. One can version control it, but that's unlikely to compress well with delta comparisons.

Using SQLite

Easy import of CSV files (with custom delimiter):

```
head -n21 amazon_reviews_us_Digital_Ebook_Purchase_v1_00.tsv > test.csv
sqlite3 test.sq3 <<EOF
.mode csv
.separator "\t"
.import test.csv test_reviews
EOF
```

The data needs some massaging to get it into CSV format—it has a few problematic characters in the dataset – let's use some shell hackery to make it uniform:

```
COLS=`head amazon_reviews_us_Digital_Ebook_Purchase_v1_00.tsv | head -n1 | sed -e 's:^\|$:":g; s:\t:", ":g'`

VALUES=`head amazon_reviews_us_Digital_Ebook_Purchase_v1_00.tsv | tail -n1 | sed -e 's:^\|$:":g; s:\t:", ":g'`

sqlite3 reviews.sq3 "create table 'aws-reviews' ( $COLS ) ;"
```

Show the tables by using the following command:

```
sqlite3 reviews.sq3 ".tables"
```

The preceding code shows the tables in the database:

```
ubuntu@commandlinebook:~$ sqlite3 reviews.sq3 ".tables"
aws-reviews
ubuntu@commandlinebook:~$
```

To show the datatypes for the table columns, run the following:

```
sqlite3 reviews.sq3 ".schema aws-reviews"
```

The preceding code produces this output:

```
ubuntu@commandlinebook:~$ sqlite3 reviews.sq3 ".schema aws-reviews"
CREATE TABLE 'aws-reviews' ( "marketplace", "customer_id", "review_id", "product_id", "product_parent", "product_title", "product_category", "star_rating", "helpful_votes", "total_votes", "vine", "verified_purchase", "review_headline", "review_body", "review_date");
ubuntu@commandlinebook:~$
```

Showing the datatypes for the table columns

Load 20 lines of Amazon reviews into the sqlite database, named `reviews.sq3`, into the `aws_reviews` table:

```
head -n21 amazon_reviews_us_Digital_Ebook_Purchase_v1_00.tsv | sed '1d;
s/"/""/g ; s/\t/", "/g;' | while read LINE ; do VALUES="\"${LINE}\"" ;
sqlite3 reviews.sq3 "insert into aws_reviews ($COLS) VALUES ($VALUES) ;";
done
```

We read the first 21 lines. Our stream editor strips the first line (the header), escapes any double-quotes with a second pair of quotes (funky escaping, we know), and replaces the "tab" delimiter with a value separator that terminates the string and indicates it has a following element.

Then we convert the read `LINE` into our input `VALUES` by prepending a double-quote and appending a double-quote to finish properly formatting our values. Finally, our data is ready to insert into the table.

Note that sqlite3 uses a second quote character as a quote-escape sequence, similar to using `%%` with `printf` to get a literal `%` character.

Now we can query the data like any traditional database, because sqlite is a database engine in library form:

```
sqlite3 reviews.sq3 "select * from aws_reviews"
```

Math in bash itself

Bash itself is able to do simple integer arithmetic. There are at least three different ways to accomplish this in bash.

Using let

You can use the let command to do simple bash arithmetic:

```
$ let x=1
$ echo $x
1
$ let x=$x+1
$ echo $x
2
```

Basic arithmetic

You can do addition, subtraction, multiplication (be sure to escape the * operator with *) and integer division:

```
expr 1 + 2
3
expr 3 \* 10
30
```

The numbers must be separated by spaces.

Double-parentheses

Similar to let, you can do simple integer arithmetic in bash using doubled parentheses:

```
a=$((1 + 2))
echo $a
((a++))
echo $a

3
4
```

To see the full range of operations available in the shell, check out the GNU reference page: https://www.gnu.org/software/bash/manual/html_node/Shell-Arithmetic.html.

bc, the unix basic calculator

bc is a calculator scripting language. Scripts in bc can be executed with the bc command. Imagine a test.bc file contains the following code:

```
scale = 2;
(10.0*2+2)/7;
```

That means you can run bc like this:

```
cat test.bc | bc
3.14
```

bc can do far more than just divide two numbers. It's a fully-fledged scripting language on its own and you can do arbitrarily complex things with a bc script. A bc script might be the ending point of a pipeline of data, where, initially, the data files are massaged into a stream of data rows, and then a bc script is used to compute the values we're looking for. Let's illustrate this with a simple example.

In this example, we need to take a CSV data file and compute the average of the second number in each row, and also compute the sum of the fourth number in each row. Say we have a bc function to compute something interesting on these two numbers, such as a harmonic mean. We can use awk to output the numbers into a bc script and then feed the result into bc using a pipe.

So, say our bc function to compute the harmonic mean of two numbers looks like this:

```
scale=5;
define harmonic(x,y){ return 2.0/((1.0/x) + (1.0/y)); }
```

We can use awk to find the two numbers and construct the bc script, and then pipe it to bc to execute:

```
awk '{s+=$2 ; f+=$4}END{print "scale=5;\n define harmonic(x,y){ return 2.0/((1.0/x) + (1.0/y)); } \n harmonic(",s/NR,",",f,")"}' data.txt | bc
```

See the bc documentation at https://www.gnu.org/software/bc/manual/html_mono/bc.html for more things you could do with bc.

SQL, Math, and Wrapping it up

Math in (g)awk

awk (including the gnu implementation, gawk) is designed to stream text processing, data extraction, and reporting. A large percentage of practical statistics is made up of counting things in specific ways, and this is one of the things awk excels at. Tallying totals, histograms, and grouped counts are all very easy in awk.

An awk program is structured as a set of patterns that are matched, and actions to take when those patterns are matched:

```
pattern {action}
pattern {action}
pattern {action}
...
```

For each record (usually each line of text passed to awk), each pattern is tested to see whether the record matches, and if so, the action is taken. Additionally, each record is automatically split into a list of fields by a delimiter. The default action, if none is given, is to print the record. The default pattern is to match everything. There are two special patterns, BEGIN and END, which are matched only before any records are processed, or after, respectively.

The power of awk lies in its variables: variables can be used without a declaration. There's some special variables already available to you that are useful for math:

```
$0: The text of the entire record.
$1, $2, … : The text of the 1st, 2nd, etc fields in the record.
NF: The number of fields in the current record.
NR: The current count of records (equal to the total number of records in
the END step)
```

Additionally, you can assign values to your own variables. awk natively supplies variables that can hold strings, integers, floating point numbers, and regular expressions and associative arrays.

As an example, say we want to count the word frequency in the reviews of our test data. Run this code:

```
zcat amazon_reviews_us_Digital_Ebook_Purchase_v1_01.tsv.gz | tail -n +2 |
head -n 10000 | cut -f14 | awk 'BEGIN {FS="[^a-zA-Z]+"}; {for
(i=1;i<NF;i++) words[$i] ++}; END {for (i in words) print words[i], i}' |
head
```

It will produce these results:

```
ubuntu@commandlinebook:~$ zcat amazon_reviews_us_Digital_Ebook_Purchase_v1_01.tsv.gz | tail -n +2 | head -n 10000 | cut -f14 | awk 'BEGIN {FS="[^a-zA-Z]+"}; {for (i=1;i<NF;i++) words[$i] ++}; END {for (i in words) print words[i], i}' | head
122
1 exuded
26 runs
12 Freda
1 Faye
1 mazing
4 Clementine
1 Mildred
1 repairing
1 graces
ubuntu@commandlinebook:~$
```

Counting the word frequency in the reviews of our test data

Say we'd like to compute a histogram of the star values of the reviews. This is also very easy with `awk`:

```
zcat amazon_reviews_us_Digital_Ebook_Purchase_v1_01.tsv.gz | tail -n +2 | cut -f8 | awk '{star[$0]++}; END {for (i in star) print i,star[i]}'
```

The preceding code produces this:

```
ubuntu@commandlinebook:~$ zcat amazon_reviews_us_Digital_Ebook_Purchase_v1_01.tsv.gz | tail -n +2 | cut -f8 | awk '{star[$0]++}; END {for (i in star) print i,star[i]}'
1 261734
2 228291
3 481927
4 1177120
5 2952621
ubuntu@commandlinebook:~$
```

Computing a histogram of the star values of the reviews

We can see that four- and five-star reviews dominate this dataset.

Besides counting, `awk` is also great for manipulating the format of strings: look back at Chapter 5, *Loops, Functions, and String Processing*, for some examples of using `awk` for string manipulation.

Python (pandas, numpy, scikit-learn)

Counting things often gets you to where you need to be, but sometimes more complex tools are required to do the job. Fortunately, we can write our own tools in the UNIX paradigm and use them in our workstream pipes along with our other command-line tools if we so desire.

One such tool is python, along with popular data science libraries such as `pandas`, `numpy`, and `scikit-learn`. This isn't a text on all the great things those libraries can do for you (if you'd like to learn, a good place to start is the official python tutorial (https://docs.python.org/3/tutorial/) and the basics of Pandas data structures in the Pandas documentation (https://pandas.pydata.org/pandas-docs/stable/basics.html). Make sure you have Python, `pip`, and `pandas` installed before you continue (see Chapter 1, *Data Science at the Command Line and Setting It Up*).

If you want to connect your python program to a piped stream however, of course there are ways to do it. A simple method is to use the `sys` library. Say we have a small pandas program tuned to our dataset that computes the mean of a couple of the columns that we know are in the data:

```
import sys
import pandas as pd

df = pd.read_csv(sys.stdin,sep='\t')
print 'star rating mean',df['star_rating'].mean()
print 'helpful votes mean', df['helpful_votes'].mean()
```

Note how we get the data directly from the `sys.stdin` stream and pass that right to pandas' `read_csv` method (using tab as a separator). If we use this method, we can pipe the data right into the script:

```
zcat amazon_reviews_us_Digital_Ebook_Purchase_v1_01.tsv.gz | head -n 100 | python average.py
```

The preceding code produces this output:

```
ubuntu@commandlinebook:~$ zcat amazon_reviews_us_Digital_Ebook_Purchase_v1_01.tsv.gz | head -n 100 | python average.py
star rating mean 4.222222222222222
helpful votes mean 1.595959595959596
ubuntu@commandlinebook:~$
```

Analyzing weather data in bash

The National Weather Service has an API to get weather data: https://forecast-v3.weather.gov/documentation. The API delivers forecast data over a lightweight HTTP interface. If you pass the correct URL and parameters to the web endpoint, the service will return JSON-formatted weather data. Let's take a look at an example of some data exploration we can do with this rich dataset.

The NWS provides both current weather data and forecasts. Let's say I'd like to see just how accurate NWS forecasts are. I'd like to do this over some amount of time, say a week. I'd like to save tomorrow's forecast, and then later on, compare those forecasts to what the temperature really was. For this example, let's look at the forecast highs, and the actual high temperatures. I'd like to do this for a single point in lat-lon.

Our overall plan will be to record the forecasts for the next day's high temperatures once a day in a CSV file. Once an hour, we'll record the actual temperature in another CSV file. Then, we'll write a script that compares these two files and computes the accuracy of each type of forecast (one-day forecast, two-day forecast, and so on) over multiple days.

First, we need to be able to query the right endpoint in the API. The weather service data is gridded into a set of grid locations. To find the grid for a particular lat-lon point, we can query the API:

```
curl -s "https://api.weather.gov/points/42.5,-71.5"
```

Querying the API returns the following:

```
{
    "@context": [
"https://raw.githubusercontent.com/geojson/geojson-ld/master/contexts/geojson-base.jsonld",

        {
            "wx": "https://api.weather.gov/ontology#",
            "s": "https://schema.org/",
            "geo": "http://www.opengis.net/ont/geosparql#",
            "unit": "http://codes.wmo.int/common/unit/",
            "@vocab": "https://api.weather.gov/ontology#",
            "geometry": {
                "@id": "s:GeoCoordinates",
                "@type": "geo:wktLiteral"
            }
    [......]
}
```

There's a lot of extraneous information in JSON, when we really only want the grid coordinates and the forecast region. Let's use the `jq` UNIX tool to parse this JSON and extract the relevant information:

```
curl -s "https://api.weather.gov/points/42.5,-71.5" | jq -r '.|
"\(.properties.cwa) \(.properties.gridX) \(.properties.gridY)"'
```

SQL, Math, and Wrapping it up

The relevant information looks like this:

```
ubuntu@commandlinebook:~$ curl -s "https://api.weather.gov/points/42.5,-71.5" | jq -r '.| "\(.properties.cwa) \(.properties.gridX) \(.properties.gridY)"'
BOX 55 80
ubuntu@commandlinebook:~$
```

Here, we've used `jq` to parse and format a bit of text that we could then insert into a URL, which we can re-curl for the forecast. Helpfully, however, the API actually gives us the entire URL of the forecast inside the JSON, in the `properties.forecastGridData` feature:

```
curl -s "https://api.weather.gov/points/42.5,-71.5" | jq -r '.|
"\(.properties.forecastGridData)"'
```

The preceding code produces this output:

```
https://api.weather.gov/gridpoints/BOX/55,80
```

We're going to take this URL, `curl` it into `jq` again, and extract the high temperature forecasts for the next day. Using `jq`, we're going to format these into a CSV line that we'll later on append to our flat file data table. For this example, we're going to ignore time zones, and assume days start and end on Zulu time. Run this code:

```
curl -s "https://api.weather.gov/gridpoints/BOX/55,80" | jq -r
'[.properties.maxTemperature.values[1].validTime[0:10],.properties.maxTempe
rature.values[1].value] | @csv'
```

It produces the following output:

```
"2018-06-22",23.88888888888897
```

 The output will be different since you're running this after 2018-06-22.

Looks great! Save this command as is to a bash script, say `forecast.sh`, using the editor of your choice. Be sure to make the script executable with the `chmod` command:

```
$ chmod 700 forecast.sh
```

And let's `cat` the file to view the contents:

```
$ cat forecast.sh
#!/bin/bash
curl -s "https://api.weather.gov/gridpoints/BOX/55,80" | jq -r
'[.properties.maxTemperature.values[1].validTime[0:10],.properties.maxTempe
rature.values[1].value] | @csv'
```

Let's add this to a cron[1] task and run this once a day at noon, and append the resulting line to a .csv file. Cron is a system utility that will run a command on a schedule. The schedules look something like this:

```
<minutes to run> <hours to run> <day of month to run> <month to run> <day
of week to run>
```

So, if we'd like to run this once a day, we want to run it on a particular minute of a particular hour, but on every day, month, and day of week giving the following cron pattern, if say, we'd like to run at noon every day:

```
0 12 * * *
```

To add a script to cron's list, the `crontab` you'll need to run the command:

crontab -e

Add the following line to your `crontab`:

```
0 12 * * * sh <script location>/forecast.sh >> <data dir>forecast.csv
```

Now, every day the forecast will be appended to the file you specified.

To get the current weather data, we need to find the closest weather station to our gridpoint:

```
curl -s "https://api.weather.gov/gridpoints/BOX/55,80/stations" | jq -r
'.observationStations[0]'
```

The preceding code produces this output:

```
https://api.weather.gov/stations/KBED
```

The current weather is located at the following API point:

```
https://api.weather.gov/stations/KBED/observations/current
```

SQL, Math, and Wrapping it up

From this API point, we can grab a timestamp and current temperature:

```
curl -s "https://api.weather.gov/stations/KBED/observations/current" | jq -r '[.properties.timestamp[0:10],.properties.temperature.value]| @csv'
"2018-06-21",20.600000000000023
```

Add this to a script file, and to your crontab as well, set to run every hour. To do this, we need to specify a minute but wildcard everything else in the cron pattern:

```
0 * * * * sh <script location>/actual.sh >> <data location>/actual.csv
```

We let this run for a couple of weeks to build our dataset.

Now, we want to take the maximum temperature we record each day, join that to the forecast we recorded for that day, and compute the difference. To find the max temperature for any given day, we can once again use `gawk`:

```
gawk   'BEGIN { FPAT = "([^,]+)|(\"[^\"]+\")" } {count[$1]++ ; max[$1] = (count[$1]==1||max[$1]<$2)?$2:max[$1]} END{ for (i in max) print $i,max[$i]}' actual.csv
"2018-06-22",18.900000000000034
```

Then, we can join this result back to our forecasts. Since the output is already sorted by date in a sortable YYYY-MM-DD order, we don't need to pre-sort. Run the following:

```
 join -t',' <(gawk   'BEGIN { FPAT = "([^,]+)|(\"[^\"]+\")" } {count[$1]++ ; max[$1] = (count[$1]==1||max[$1]<$2)?$2:max[$1]} END{ for (i in max) print $i,max[$i]}' actual.csv ) forecast.csv
```

The preceding code produces the following output:

```
"2018-06-22",18.900000000000034 ,23.88888888888897
...
```

And we can pipe this stream to `awk` to compute the difference between the actual and predicted temperatures:

```
> join -t',' <(gawk   'BEGIN { FPAT = "([^,]+)|(\"[^\"]+\")" } {count[$1]++ ; max[$1] = (count[$1]==1||max[$1]<$2)?$2:max[$1]} END{ for (i in max) print $i,max[$i]}' actual.csv ) forecast.csv | gawk 'BEGIN { FPAT = "([^,]+)|(\"[^\"]+\")" } {print $1,$2-$3}'
```

The preceding code results in the following:

```
"2018-06-22" -4.98889
```

We grabbed real data from the Internet, massaged it using a workflow, stored it into files, and computed numeric values with the data in the tables we made!

Summary

In this chapter, we used `cut`, `grep`, `awk`, and `sort` to deeply inspect our data, as one would in a more traditional database. We then saw how sqlite can provide a lightweight alternative to other databases. Using these tools together, we were able to mine useful knowledge from our raw files.

We also saw how the command line offers several options for doing arithmetic and other mathematical operations. Simple arithmetic and grouped tallies can be performed using bash itself or `awk`. More complex mathematics can be done using a scripting language, such as `bc` or python, and be called like other command-line workflow tools.

Finally, we used many of the tools we discussed to produce a useful and interesting result from publicly-available data.

We hope that this book broadens your understanding of just how powerful the command line actually is, especially for data science. However, this is only the very beginning. There's a number of tools and other commands we haven't even mentioned, which are very powerful and deserve to be mentioned. BashHTTPD (https://github.com/avleen/bashttpd) is a web server in bash; it may sound silly, but the shell can really do amazing things. BashReduce (https://github.com/erikfrey/bashreduce) gives the user the ability to run bash commands over multiple machines/cores. You might have noticed some of the commands took a little while to run. We recommend taking a look at BashReduce to speed things up. Those who are familiar with the MapReduce concept should have no issue picking up and working with BashReduce.

We also want to mention that there are so many other great command-line tools out there; we could write about them forever. However, for this book, we decided to focus on the everyday commands and provide examples on how to use them. We hope you enjoyed this book!

Other Books You May Enjoy

If you enjoyed this book, you may be interested in these other books by Packt:

Beginning Data Science with Python and Jupyter
Alex Galea

ISBN: 9781789532029

- Identify potential areas of investigation and perform exploratory data analysis
- Plan a machine learning classification strategy and train classification models
- Use validation curves and dimensionality reduction to tune and enhance your models
- Scrape tabular data from web pages and transform it into Pandas DataFrames
- Create interactive, web-friendly visualizations to clearly communicate your findings

Hands-On Data Science with Anaconda
Dr. Yuxing Yan

ISBN: 9781788831192

- Perform cleaning, sorting, classification, clustering, regression, and dataset modeling using Anaconda
- Use the package manager conda and discover, install, and use functionally efficient and scalable packages
- Get comfortable with heterogeneous data exploration using multiple languages within a project
- Perform distributed computing and use Anaconda Accelerate to optimize computational powers
- Discover and share packages, notebooks, and environments, and use shared project drives on Anaconda Cloud
- Tackle advanced data prediction problems

Leave a review - let other readers know what you think

Please share your thoughts on this book with others by leaving a review on the site that you bought it from. If you purchased the book from Amazon, please leave us an honest review on this book's Amazon page. This is vital so that other potential readers can see and use your unbiased opinion to make purchasing decisions, we can understand what our customers think about our products, and our authors can see your feedback on the title that they have worked with Packt to create. It will only take a few minutes of your time, but is valuable to other potential customers, our authors, and Packt. Thank you!

Index

A

advanced shell scripting
   about 53
   complex utility functions 53
   text injection, of text files 53, 54
Ammonite
   reference 8
append operator 74
awk
   about 80, 81, 82, 98, 99
   reference 82

B

Bash networks 54, 55
bash
   weather data, analyzing 100, 101, 102, 103, 104
basic arithmetic
   performing 96
bc command 97
book data
   example 59, 60, 61
Bourne-again shell (bash) 8
bracket expansions
   reference 68

C

case statement 72
cd command 23
columnar
   data, viewing as 88, 89
command line
   history 6, 7
   navigating 26, 27
   need for 9, 10
   setting up, on OS X 16, 18
   setting up, on Ubuntu Linux 18, 19
   setting up, with Docker 19
   setting up, with Windows 10 11, 12, 13, 14, 16
commands
   basics 21, 22, 23, 24, 25, 26
   locating 22
cut command 37, 38, 88, 89, 90

D

data
   downloading 32
   viewing, as columnar 88, 89
detached processing 39
Docker
   command line, setting up with 19
dot character 77
doubled parentheses
   using 96

F

file command
   using 33, 34
for loops 68
Friendly Interactive Shell (fish) 8

G

gnuplot
   using 56
grep 75
GROUP BY operation 92, 93

H

help
   obtaining 28, 29
heredoc operator 75

I

IFS (internal field separator) 49

J

join command 91

L

language-focused shells 8
let command
    using, for bash arithmetic 96
loops
    about 68, 69
    for loop 68
    until construct 72
    while loop 70
ls command 22

N

numpy 100

O

operations research 9
OS X
    command line, setting up on 16, 18
output redirection operator 73, 74

P

pandas
    reference 100
pipe character 78
positional parameters 51
POSIX (Portable Operating System Interface) 21
process
    running, in background 40
pwd command 22
python
    reference 100

R

regular expressions
    about 75
    character sets 76, 77
    dot character 77
    exact matches 76
    groups, capturing 78
    operators 79
    pipe character 78
    repetitions, matching 79

S

scikit-learn 100
screen 41, 42
screen session
    sharing, between multiple users 44
sed
    about 82
    reference 83
selects
    simulating 93
shebang 49
shell script
    about 48
    function arguments 49, 50
    IFS (internal field separator) 52
    positional parameters 51
    shebang 48
shell
    customizing 30
SIGHUP 41
sort command 25, 83, 84, 85
SQLite
    about 94
    using 94, 95

T

Terminal
    output 63
    stacked bar chart output 65
    text-based output 64
    working with 56, 58, 59
tmux 44, 46
top command 43
tr command 83
tsv (tab separated values) 37

U

Ubuntu Linux
    command line, setting up on 18, 19

uniq command 25, 85
until construct 72

W

WHERE clauses 90
while loop 70
Windows 10

command line, setting up with 11, 12, 13, 14, 16
word count
 performing 35, 36

X

Xonsh
 reference 8

Printed in Germany
by Amazon Distribution
GmbH, Leipzig